01-1

HOW IT HAPPENED

By the same author:

A Short History of Farming (Macmillan, 1970)

What They've said about Nineteenth Century Reformers (Oxford University Press, 1971)

HOW IT HAPPENED

Frank E. Huggett

BASIL BLACKWELL · OXFORD

0 631 14040 9

Printed by offset in Great Britain by
William Clowes & Sons, Limited
London, Beccles and Colchester

CONTENTS

ACKNOWLEDGEMENTS

The author and publishers wish to thank the following for permission to use copyright pictures:

The BBC, *Crystal Set*; The Central Office of Information, *Open Prison*; The Central Press, *Festival of Youth*; The GLC, *Cheapside 1900, Tooting Bathing Pond, Albury Street 1911, Blackheath School 1906, Albion Street School 1908*; The GPO, *Women Clerks*; The Illustrated London News, *London, Main Drainage*; The Imperial War Museum, *Pillbox*; The Library Association, *Eastbourne Public Library*; The Mansell Collection, *Honeymoon 3rd Class, Bathing at Ramsgate, A Fleet Wedding, Cheapside XVIIIth Century, Lord Hardwicke, Bride and Sweep, Coffee Stall, Cheapside 1846, A 'Peeler', Robert Raikes, Left in Charge, Our Little Brother, Woman Spinning 1814, A Weaver's Home, Vaccination, The Watch House, The Battle of Albuera, Bathing at Bridlington, Street Breakfast, The Coffee House, Gretna Marriage Certificate, Victorian Wedding, Leap Frog, The Young Housemaid, A London Slum*; The MCC, *England v. Australia Test, Brading, Ladies' Cricket Match*; The Radio Times Hulton Picture Library, *Heart and Lung Machine, An Early Operation*; Rex Smith, *Nippy*; Tit-Bits, *Photograph of First Issue*; The Wellcome Institute, *The Climbing Boy, Save the Babies, Dr. Barnardo's Festival, Child Apprentices, St. Bartholomew's, Ward at Scutari, Infant Nursery, The Foundling Hospital, Barber's Shop Operation*.

The Chimney Sweep and his climbing Boy.
For a few coppers, the sweep obtains a new recruit from a poor mother.

Child apprentices.
In 1840 poor children still supplemented their scanty rations from the pig trough.

Blackheath School, 1906.
A drill class in the hall.

1. BIRTH AND EDUCATION

The Georgian Age

Just over 200 years ago, babies had only a fifty-fifty chance of living beyond their first birthday. It has been estimated that in the years from 1741 to 1750, about 430 children out of every 1,000 born, died before they were one year old, many of them in the first few weeks of life.

To help bring children into the world there were in most parts of the country still only ignorant female midwives, who had no medical training, but only a vast stock of 'magic' remedies handed down from generation to generation. In difficult births some midwives placed a special girdle, embroidered with mystic figures and signs, around the woman's stomach. Since the sixteenth century, it had been necessary for official midwives to have a Bishop's licence. This licence, which cost 18s. 4d., was granted only to women who agreed not to give abortions and not to substitute one child for another. But the main qualification for midwives was that they should be good Christian women, for many of the children they brought into the world left it again so speedily, that they often had to carry out instant baptisms. Midwives did not know how to prevent these babies from dying; all they could do was to ensure that their souls went to Heaven.

When a woman—rich or poor—was about to have a baby, the midwife and, usually, the woman's friends were called in. Their main concern was to see that the mother did not catch cold. If she could afford it, a fire was lit in the room and she was given large quantities of gin or brandy to help her to forget the pains of labour.

According to W. Cadogan, a contemporary writer: 'As soon as she is delivered, if the person is in affluent circumstances, she is covered up close in bed with additional clothes, the curtains are drawn round the bed, and pinned together, every crevice in the window and door is stopped close, not excepting even the keyhole, the windows are guarded not only with shutters and curtains, but even with blankets, the more

effectually to exclude the fresh air, and the good woman is not suffered to put her arm, or even her nose out of bed, for fear of catching cold. She is constantly supplied out of the spout of a tea-pot with large quantities of warm liquors, to keep up perspiration and sweat, and her whole diet consists of them.'

If after a few days she started to shiver or show any signs of catching cold, 'more clothes are heaped upon her; spirituous liquors, and hot spices, are given her, to throw off the cold fit.' This sometimes went on for many days.

The poor people living in the towns fared no better. In most cases they could not afford to light a fire—even if they had a fireplace—and they had no spare clothes to heap upon themselves.

Having a baby was an expensive business. Some farm labourers' budgets, collected by the Rev. David Davies in 1787, showed that they had to spend on 'the child's linen, 3s. or 4s.; the midwife's fee, 5s.; a bottle of gin or brandy always had upon this occasion, 2s.; attendance of a nurse for a few days, and her diet, at least 5s.; half a bushel of malt brewed, and hops, 3s.; to the minister for churching, 1s.' And the average wage of a farm worker at that time was only about 6s. a week.

But in one way at least the children of the poor had a better chance of surviving than those of the rich. At birth, children were wrapped tightly in flannel bandages. These swaddling clothes were designed—in accordance with current medical theory—to keep the bad air out and the nourishing juices in. But the children of the rich were so copiously wrapped in flannel bandages and clothes that they sometimes weighed as much as the baby itself. Baby girls were frequently laced up in stays to give them the favoured 'sugarloaf' shape. In addition, directly the baby was born it was usual 'to cram a dab of butter and sugar down its throat', or a little oil or bread pulp. Another widespread custom among the rich was to give it a piece of roast pork 'to cure it of all the mother's longings'.

Many rich mothers did not feed the baby themselves, but employed another woman— a wet nurse—to do so. Wet nurses were paid as much as ten guineas a quarter—a very high wage in those days: a serving girl received about £3 a year. Partly, perhaps, because of this expense, but even more through ignorance, rich children were weaned very early, often at three months of age. They were fed on pieces of chicken, chicken broth, on rich cakes and sweetmeats, and on bread pulp, enriched with sugar, spices, and sometimes even a drop of wine. They were fed every time they cried, sometimes more than 12 times in a day, and they were made to eat until they were sick.

But the underfeeding of the poor was just as fatal as the overfeeding of the rich; and both rich and poor were exposed to all the deadly plagues of smallpox and other diseases which were so common at that time.

The children who had the least chance of surviving were those abandoned by their mothers or brought up in the parish workhouse. Under the Elizabethan Poor Law Acts of 1598 to 1601, each parish was obliged to support the old, the sick, the poor and their children. The poor law was administered by overseers, appointed by the local justices of the peace for one year, and the churchwardens. The overseers collected the poor rate from the residents who could afford to pay it. These ratepayers were naturally concerned that the poor rate should be as low as possible and most overseers tried to spend as little money on relief as possible. By the second half of the eighteenth century the system had begun to break down. This was largely owing to the increase in population, which in England and Wales almost doubled during the eighteenth century, rising from an estimated 5½ million to 9 million.

Poor law relief was usually provided only by the parish in which a person had been born. Later acts of Parliament gave the justices and overseers power to send back those in need to their original parish. One of the main aims of some overseers was to hustle out of the parish any unmarried mothers-to-

be so that the child would not become a burden upon the parish poor rate by having been born there. For, not only would there be all the expenses of confinement—even pauper women lay in bed for many days after having a baby—but the additional burden of supporting the child until it could be apprenticed to some trade.

Unmarried mothers who were living in parishes other than their own, or who fled to a different part of the country, were frequently 'tied to the end of a cart naked' and whipped till their bodies 'be bloody by reason of such whipping' before they were sent back as vagrants to their own parish. Many unmarried mothers abandoned their babies or killed them. They then often trudged off to the nearest big city where they could find lucrative employment in feeding another woman's baby as a wet nurse. The babies they had abandoned were taken to the parish poorhouse or 'cared for' by nurses in the parish. Few of the babies lived long. Out of 10,000 babies taken in by the Dublin Foundling Asylum between 1775 and 1796 only 45 survived. The death rate in other asylums was little different.

Having a baby often resulted in great suffering. This suffering was caused not so much perhaps through cruelty, as through ignorance. The standard of values then was quite different from those of today. Poverty, in a nation where something like half the people did not earn enough to live on and had to be supported by the poor rates, was accepted as inevitable. Children's deaths were accepted in the same way, as no one knew how to prevent them. Nevertheless, there were a number of individuals who were concerned by this suffering, and even the government would have cured it if it had known how to do so.

One of these individuals was Thomas Coram, a shipmaster who had gone to America as a young man. On his return to England he was so affected by the sight of abandoned children in the Rotherhithe district and the stories of the poor, demented mothers killing their unwanted babies, that he petitioned George II for a charter to open a Foundling Hospital.

When the charter was granted, a board of governors was set up under the Duke of Bedford. The hospital was financed by subscriptions from the wealthy. It was built at Lamb's Conduit Fields, then on the edge of London. The hospital was fantastically successful. Between 1741, when it opened, and 1756, only half of the 1,384 children admitted to the hospital died. Greatly impressed by what had been achieved, the government agreed in 1756 to subsidise the hospital on condition that all unwanted babies under the age of two months were admitted.

On June 2, 1756, a wicker basket was hung at the gates, in which the children could be placed. So great was the need that on the first day 171 babies were placed in the basket—double the number that had been admitted in the whole of any previous year. Social security then was organised locally, not nationally, and all over the country, parish overseers seized upon this chance to relieve the poor rate of their infant burdens at the government's expense.

The overseers sometimes gave the babies to vagrants who, for a small sum of money, took them to the Foundling Hospital in London. Some of the babies never arrived there. In one case, a vagrant got drunk on the way to London, slept out in the open, and woke in the morning to find three of his five small charges dead through exposure. Many of the babies were placed in the basket naked, their few ragged clothes having been stolen by the man who had brought them, to be sold on the flourishing second-hand clothes market in London for the price of a few nips of gin.

It was the government's regulation that any baby should be admitted that proved fatal to the hospital's success. The hospital became so overcrowded and so many of the babies were weak and ill upon arrival that the death rate leapt up to 70 per cent. After four years the government withdrew its subsidy; but the venture had shown what could have been achieved if there had been enough

The Foundling Hospital, London. *Mothers arriving with their unwanted babies.*

national wealth for all children to be cared for adequately.

There was also some public pressure for the government to stop its subsidy. The hospital was being used not only by the poor for whom it had originally been intended, but also by unmarried rich girls, who used it as a convenient dumping ground for their unwanted babies. It was possibly some society girl who pinned the following verses to her baby's clothes before it was left in the wicker basket:

Go, gentle babe, thy future life be spent
In virtuous purity, and calm content;
Life's sunshine bless thee, and no anxious care
Sit on thy brow, and draw the falling tear;
Thy country's grateful servant may'st thou prove
And all thy life be happiness and love.

Some of the society girls' babies were quite well dressed as the admission list for 1741 showed:

A male child, about two months old, with white dimity sleeves,* lined with white, and tied with red ribbon.
A female child, aged about six weeks, with a blue figured ribbon, and purple and white printed linen sleeves, turned up with red and white.

* A garment made of stout cotton fabric.

A male child, about a fortnight old, very neatly dressed; a fine holland cap, with a cambric border, white corded dimity sleeves, the shirt ruffled with cambric.

Babies and children of the poor were not dressed in that way. The children usually wore clothes which had been handed down from an older brother or sister or cut down from their parents' clothes. Their clothes were often made of corduroy or thick, heavy wool. Many of the children living in the towns dressed in rags and ran about barefooted. Clothes were sometimes patched and darned until they fell apart.

Almost as soon as they could walk, children were expected to help keep themselves by working. George Crompton, the eldest son of the man who invented the spinning mule, recalled that 'soon after I was able to walk I was employed in cotton manufacture'. He had to help his mother at home by treading down the wet cotton in a large brown tub. When the tub 'became so full that I could no longer safely stand on it, a chair was placed beside it, and I held on by the back'. Other boys and girls of four or five earned a few pence each week by scaring birds off the growing crops or by stopping cattle from straying.

It was the pauper children who often had the hardest time. At the age of seven, or sometimes before, the workhouse overseers would apprentice them to some tradesman or farmer. The boys' apprenticeship lasted till the age of 24 and the girls' till 21 or marriage. In theory, they should have been taught a useful trade and have been clothed and fed by their master. In fact, pauper apprentices were more often starved, beaten and so brutally treated that they ran away to join the vast bands of vagrant children who thronged the muddy roads of the country and the dark, insanitary alleys of the cities.

But during this period, conditions for children did begin to improve. For a start, their chances of survival began to increase. In the middle of the eighteenth century, it was still common for a woman to have ten

children, of whom five might die before they were one year old and another two or three before they were five. But a group of pioneer obstetricians—man-midwives as they were then called—began to show, through their practice and their teaching, how babies' lives could be prolonged. Such men as William Smellie, Charles White, Sir Richard Manningham, and John and William Hunter started to deal with the problems of childbirth in a completely new way.

They let women get up two days after they had had a child, instead of confining them to bed for weeks; they kept the room well ventilated and cool; and they insisted on greater personal cleanliness and hospital hygiene by closing the wards for two or three months every year, even though their reasons for doing so were mistaken. The first hospital for Poor Lying-in Women in Great Britain was opened in Dublin by Bartholomew Mosse in 1745. Four years later, the British Lying-in Hospital was opened in London; in 1915 it merged with another hospital to form a new British Hospital for Mothers and Babies which still exists at Woolwich. In 1752 the General Lying-in Hospital, which later came under the patronage of Queen Charlotte, was founded.

During this period, too, the education of poor children was not entirely neglected. Throughout the eighteenth century, more and more charity schools were opened. These were financed by subscriptions from the middle classes and the rich. Some schools even paid the poor child's parents a few pennies each week to compensate for the loss of their children's earnings.

School hours were long. The pupils usually started work between five and seven in the morning and did not finish until seven or eight at night. Not all of the time was taken up by lessons; they were also usefully and profitably employed in spinning or knitting or some other craft. Although some of the better pupils were taught to write or even to do sums, most learnt little more than how to read.

The main purpose was to make the children God-fearing, honest citizens, capable of reading the Bible. Lessons were learnt by rote from catechisms, such as the one published towards the end of the eighteenth century, which included the following questions and answers:

Q—What shall become of you if you die in your sin?
A—I must go to hell with the wicked.
Q—What kind of place is hell?
A—A place of endless torment, being a lake that burns with fire and brimstone.
Q—Who are the wicked that go to hell at death?
A—Such as refuse Christ, neglect to read God's word, and pray to him; or who lie, steal, curse, swear, profane the Sabbath, and disobey their parents.

In many parts of the country, there were 'dame's schools', often run by curates to supplement their small incomes, where for a few pennies a week, children might learn to read. And towards the end of the century, Sunday schools were set up in many of the towns, where children went for one day a week—usually from 9 a.m. to 6 p.m.—to sing hymns, to learn to read, and to attend church or chapel.

Although Sunday schools had existed previously in other places such as Macclesfield and Ashbury, Berks., it was the one set up in Gloucester which really got the Sunday school movement under way. It was opened by Robert Raikes, a newspaper editor and printer, and the Rev. Thomas Stock in St. Catherine Street, Gloucester, in 1780. Any child no matter how ragged, could attend; the only qualification in Raikes's own words were that children should have 'clean hands, clean faces, and hair combed'.

Although Sunday schools were to teach so many millions of children to read, education was not their main purpose. It was, again in Raikes's words 'to check the deplorable profanation of the Sabbath' by stopping children from playing in the streets. The idea was eagerly seized upon by others. John Wesley,

Left in Charge.
Two children watch over the baby in its cradle.

Leapfrog has been a popular game in all ages.

the founder of the Methodist Church, was one of the first to recognise the importance of Sunday schools in restraining children from 'open sin' and teaching them 'a little good manners, at least, as well as to read the Bible'. Although the original purpose of the Sunday schools was not so much education as keeping the Sabbath holy, they did achieve a great success in teaching thousands of children to read who, without this instruction, would have remained illiterate.

Infant Nursery.
Conditions for children had not improved much by the middle of the nineteenth century.

Robert Raikes.
The main founder of the Sunday school movement.

The Years of Growth

Progress in the education and care of children did not continue uninterrupted. From the start of the industrial revolution children had been employed in factories. They could operate the machines just as well as, and far more cheaply than, adults could. As more and more factories opened in the towns, the number of children employed in them also grew. Parents sent their young sons and daughters into the cotton mills, the potteries and the coal mines to obtain the work that they sometimes could not get themselves. Parish overseers in all parts of the country sent workhouse children to the mills in waggonloads.

Amongst one group of 80 boys and girls of seven years of age sent as apprentices from St. Pancras workhouse in London to a mill ten miles from Nottingham was Robert Blincoe. In 1832 he described 'the horrors' of his earlier experiences. The boys wore rough shirts and trousers and the girls pinafores 'made of coarse linen that reached from the neck to the heels'. Their working clothes were stained with grease, as also were the beds in which they slept—in pairs. They had a breakfast of black bread and porridge at 5 a.m. and started work, half an hour later, sometimes working through the dinner hour and not finishing until 7 p.m.

His first job, before he started to work on the machines, was to pick up loose cotton from the floor. He was half suffocated by the 'dust and flue'. In some ways it was worse than the workhouse, for there at least they had not been overworked and when they ate their meagre meals the table had been covered with a tablecloth and a salt cellar had been provided, even though salt was still a precious commodity. At the mill they had neither salt nor tablecloth.

Even so the mill was better than many others. 'They were kept decently clad, had a bettermost suit reserved for Sundays and holidays—were occasionally allowed a little time for play, in the open air, and upon Goose-fair day, which is, or then was, a great festival at Nottingham—the whole of them were conveyed in carts to that celebrated place, and regaled with furmenty* and sixpence in money was allowed to the very youngest! They went pretty regularly to Lowdham Church on Sunday; were not confined within the gates and walls as was the case at most other mills, where parish apprentices were immured!' But conditions were much worse at the second mill he went to after the first one had closed. They often had to work 16 hours a day, were brutally beaten, and some of them were injured in the unguarded machines. The highlight of their week was Sunday dinner, which consisted of a few scraps of boiled Irish bacon and unpeeled turnips.

Even by the beginning of the nineteenth century, however, laws were being passed to make their lives a little better. In 1802, the first Factory Act was passed, limiting the hours of work of poorhouse children in cotton mills to 12 a day, of which part should be used to teach them reading, writing and arithmetic. But there was no one to see that the law was carried out until another Factory Act was passed in 1833 appointing factory inspectors.

Conditions were just as bad, and in some ways more frightening, for the boys and girls working in coal mines. Seven or eight was the normal age for them to start work underground, but some were sent down at four or five. The youngest children were employed as 'trappers', crouching in the dark for 12 or 14 hours a day beside a ventilation door in the pit which they had to open and shut as coal tubs rattled through. Some worked as 'hurryers', pushing or pulling loaded tubs in narrow seams where all but children were too big to go. Others had to carry creels, or baskets of coal up a flight of winding, rickety steps to the pithead. But in 1842 women, girls and boys under 10 were prohibited by law from working underground.

The worst fate of all was reserved for those

* Wheat, with the husk removed, boiled in milk: with sugar and spices, such as cinnamon.

children apprenticed to chimney sweeps. They had to climb up the chimneys to sweep them. Their limbs and bodies were scratched and bruised; their mouths and noses were filled with soot; and there was the ever-present danger of getting stuck—and dying —in one of the flues. The practice did not really start to die out until 1864 when a law was passed sentencing to hard labour any master who employed a climbing boy. Even then there were still some evasions; the last death of a climbing boy occurred in Cambridge in February, 1875.

Not all masters or all factories ill-treated their child-workers. And not all children were living or working in the towns, where the worst conditions and the hardest jobs were to be found. But even for children living in some parts of the country, life probably became somewhat harder in the first half of the nineteenth century. The increase in the size of farms and different farming methods —particularly the growing of turnips in the eastern counties—created a need for a large labour force at certain times of the year. Here again it was cheaper to employ children than adults. When help was needed on the farms a gangmaster would hire all the children he could for a few pence each per day and let them out on contract to the highest bidder. The children were gathered together early in the morning—sometimes at 4 a.m.—and marched off to the farm, which was sometimes miles away. There they were employed in tasks such as picking fruit, thinning turnips, weeding and spreading manure. Often they did not get back home until 10 at night. Many of them were only six or seven years of age. It was not until 1867 that a law was passed making it illegal for children under eight to be employed in these agricultural gangs and even in the 1890s some critics claimed that the law was still being evaded.

It was the greater national wealth that children's work had helped in part to produce which gave an opportunity for their better treatment. Before the nineteenth century it had been generally accepted, and expected, that children should work to help keep themselves. There was little superfluous wealth to allow them to be clothed and fed while they were educated. When the factories opened, it seemed only natural that the town children should operate the new machines while country children were plaiting straw or spinning wool in their cottages. But the greater public exposure of the hardships of child labour, and the more dangerous and unhealthy nature of the tasks they were called upon to do, produced a change of attitude towards children, first of all among a few reformers, and then more generally. And as national wealth increased it became more possible for individuals, the Church and finally the State itself to devote money to their education.

At the beginning of the period there were three main kinds of school to which an ordinary child might go: a dame's school; a Sunday school, whose number had increased to over 5,000, with 452,000 pupils, by 1818; or one of the old charity schools or new church schools, established by such voluntary bodies as the Church of England's National Society, founded in 1811. By 1833, the National Society had established about 7,000 schools, catering for half a million pupils.

In the dame's school the method of instruction was the same as it had been for many years. Alexander Somerville, the son of a Scottish farm labourer, described in his autobiography his first days at the village school he went to in 1818. The school was at Birnynows, 'a hamlet of about twenty houses, forming a kind of square fifty yards wide, the square filled with pigstyes, dunghills, stagnant pools, and stacks of firewood. The houses in the square were all miserable thatched sheds . . . One of the oldest and most infirm of the thatched houses was the school room. The school-master was a lame man, and was a teacher only because he was lame . . . So, my education, having got a twopenny spelling book, began. The first six weeks were consumed in learning to forget to name the letters as my father and mother had named them. . . .'

At this school, they were taught not only reading and spelling, but also writing and some arithmetic. They started with the Tyro's Guide. They then progressed to the Bible and a Spelling and Pronouncing Cathecism by Alexander Barrie, which had first been published 22 years before. Discipline was harsh. One day when Alexander was late for school, the schoolmaster asked him why he was late. Alexander's reply offended the schoolmaster 'upon which he took his great leathern belt, thirty inches long, two and a half inches broad, which was split half way up with six thongs, the end of each having been burned in the fire to make it hard; the other end of the belt having a slit in it, into which he put his hand and wound it round his wrist. With this instrument, called the *taws*, he thrashed me on the hands, head, face, neck, shoulders, back, legs, everywhere, until I was blistered.'

But there were rewards as well as punishments. On Friday, the boys and girls re-read all the lessons they had learnt during the week and said the week's spelling lessons over again. 'The teacher kept slates with every pupil's name written on them, and against each name, he, during the week, put a mark for being too late to school, for being deficient in any lesson, or hymn, or question; and on the Friday he put a mark for each mistake in reading or spelling.' A junior pupil with no marks against his name was given $\frac{1}{2}d.$ and a senior pupil, 1$d.$

There was so great a demand for education and so few teachers that some more economical method of instruction was required. This was provided by the so-called Madras method, which had first been used extensively in India by the Rev. Andrew Bell. As superintendent of the Madras Male Orphan Asylum, he had used the older pupils there to instruct the younger.

The system worked so well that on his return to England he published a book describing it. Although the method had been used to a limited extent in charity and Sunday schools in the eighteenth century, it was now seized upon by the many schoolmasters who found themselves with large classes and no one to teach the pupils. One of the first to take up the new method at the beginning of the century was Joseph Lancaster, a Quaker, who expanded his school for the poor in Borough Road, Southwark, until it contained 1,000 pupils.

Under the Madras system, the better pupils taught the worst. First, the alphabet was learnt by writing in sand. Then the pupils went on to read simple words and finally whole sentences, such as: 'The dog is trying to bite the bear. It is very cruel to set dogs to torture any other animals, and I hope as you grow old you will endeavour to prevent cruelty, as it is wicked to encourage such practices.'

The Madras, or monitorial, system of education has been criticised for being mechanical and rigid—but so was much of the other education at that time. In fact, in the hands of many of the teachers, it became a method of education which was far in advance of its time; it is only now that some of the basic principles are being used again by progressive teachers in primary schools. Because it was economical with teachers, it allowed the size of classes to be kept down to 24 pupils, or 36 at the most. It established a principle of mutual aid, with the 12 best pupils in the class sitting by the side of the 12 worst, and helping them to learn their lessons and being responsible for their conduct and their progress. And associated with it was a desire to let children govern themselves and to replace the brutal beatings of the dame's schools by more humane punishments.

George Reynolds, master of Lambeth School and writing master to the Female Asylum, Lambeth, published a pamphlet in 1813 explaining how he used the Madras method in his own school. A register of offences was kept in a Black Book, inspected in the presence of the whole school once a week. Offenders were tried by a jury of peers —that is 'twelve of the best boys, selected for that purpose, and a verdict pronounced by them on the accused'. The main method of punishment was wearing 'a badge of dis-

grace . . . made of double block tin and hung with a small iron chain around the neck and suspended loosely in front'—a far less severe punishment than that used in many dame's schools.

Even those parents who wanted to send their children to school could not always find one. In 1818, over a quarter of the parishes in England had no school of any kind—not even a dame's school. And very few of the dame's schools and not all of the charity, or voluntary, schools were free. Though the 'fees' were only a few pence a week, many parents could not afford even that small amount. Alexander Somerville had to wait until the price of food became lower in 1818 and his parents could afford to buy him some clothes to replace his rags, before he could go to school. His sister went with him, too, but only for a quarter of the year before she had to go and work in the fields; and he himself left in the following summer to help a farmer look after his cows, though he went back to school again the following winter.

Because of the lack of education, many adults could not read, and fewer still could write. In the middle of the nineteenth century, 40 per cent of the adult population could not sign their name and even by the 1880s there were 20 per cent who could not do so.

Attitudes towards education were, however, changing. As trade increased there was a demand, particularly in the large cities, for more workers who could read and write and do sums. Employers wanted clerks who could write fast, not merely copy words painfully and slowly. To cater for this demand, some enterprising publishers started to produce books around the middle of the nineteenth century to teach both children and adults the new favoured style. One was called *Farnell's Rapid Writer—or Young Gentlemen's and Lady's Complete Running-Hand System.* It was claimed to be 'the only plan ever published that practically breaks from the School Copy book to the Epistolatory, Law, and Merchant's Running Hand Style. Perfect for adult self-instruction . . . . One week's steady and continued practice on this superior system, will fit a bad writer to occupy respectably a position at the Merchant's desk.'

The need for self-instruction in writing was soon to disappear. In 1870 an Education Act was passed which made it obligatory for schools to be set up in places where there was not one already. Ten years later it was made compulsory for the new school boards to see that children went to school at five and stayed there until the age of 10, when they might leave if they had reached a certain standard of education. In cities and towns throughout the country new Board schools were built—those ornately-decorated, red or yellow brick schools with their stone staircases and rough wooden floors, a few of which are still in use to this day. The building housed both the infants' school and the elementary school, divided into separate sections for boys and girls.

Some of the children went to school before they were five. At the age of seven, they were transferred from the infants' to the elementary school—if they could read, spell, write and do little sums. The children sat on wooden forms and wrote on slates. Their education did not last for long, as most of them still left school at the age of 10.

Nevertheless, this was to produce a complete change in attitude towards education. It was now accepted that all children should receive full-time education at least until the age of 10. And there were many homes where parents wished that their children could continue doing so even longer.

Modern Times

The attitude towards children has changed completely in recent times. Formerly, they were treated as miniature adults: to be fed the same food from an early age; to be dressed in cut-down clothes of their parents; and to be sent to work, like adults, as soon as possible. It was not considered necessary to allow children a long period of time in which to develop their minds, personalities and skills. Such an idea, however, could scarcely have arisen while so many children died when they were young. And even if more children had lived longer, there was still not sufficient national wealth to allow all of them to be well fed, cared for and educated until they were grown up.

In modern times, better food and advances in medical science have allowed more children to survive, while increased national wealth has permitted more and more of them to stay on at school for increasingly longer periods. Children have become important in their own right. The change in their status has been so great that even by

'Our Little Brother'.
The baby carriage made it easier for children to take their little brothers out.

Our Little Brother.

the beginning of the present century some writers were beginning to complain of 'the century of the child in which the children are always right and parents and teachers are always wrong'.

There has been just as great a change in the care of babies. During the modern period more and more mothers have come to feed their babies with a bottle. In the sixteenth century a very few babies had been artificially fed—from a cow's horn or a spoon. Then, towards the end of the eighteenth century, the 'bubby pot' was invented for feeding children. It was usually made of pewter and was shaped like a beer tankard or a gravy pot with a long spout. During the first half of the nineteenth century, feeding bottles similar in shape to those of today were produced. They were made of porcelain, but towards the end of the nineteenth century, glass bottles were increasingly used. In 1900 the first infant feeding bottle incorporating the modern teat and valve—the Allenbury's feeder—was manufactured.

At first, many mothers fed their babies on condensed sweetened milk, which had started to appear in the shops in the 1870s. This milk was quite unsuitable for babies as it lacked fat and some of the vitamins necessary for growth. But at that time it was no more harmful than cow's milk which was often infected with tuberculosis germs.

It was not until the 1890s that some people started to boil milk—and the baby's bottle—to make them safe. Right up to the First World War most people still collected their milk in jugs or bowls from a dairyman with his open churn in the streets. Pasteurised milk in sealed glass bottles started to be delivered to the door in the 1920s.

Babies were no longer wrapped tightly in swaddling clothes, though some doctors still advised that a flannel binder should be wrapped around the stomach of the newborn baby 'and should be worn, especially in cold and damp weather, until after the second teething is past'. Baby carriages, or perambulators, as they were then called, had been in use in the first half of the nineteenth

century; some were made of wood and had only three wheels.

The pram had at first a number of critics. The writer of one book on the domestic management of children, published in 1874, said that it was 'a modern convenience, injurious to the child, though approved of by nurses'. He recommended that children should be taken for short walks, and be carried at intervals when tired. In spite of these criticisms, the pram became popular amongst all classes, particularly when the paving of more city and country roads permitted its wider use. In the second half of the nineteenth century more than a dozen big manufacturers began to produce prams in Britain.

At the beginning of the period, many babies and young children were still dying from diphtheria, dysentery and other diseases. In 1900, 154 out of every 1,000 babies born in England and Wales still never lived to see their first birthday. In desperation, many mothers turned to patent medicines, such as Fenning's Fever Curer, which was a popular remedy at the beginning of this century. The makers claimed that typhus, or low fever, could be cured with two doses, diphtheria with three, scarlet fever with four and dysentery with five. Deaths among young children did start to fall around 1900, though it was not due to these medicines, but to better food and housing, increased medical knowledge and the provision of infant welfare centres.

The death rate amongst babies was particularly high in London; at some periods of the year one in five babies died before they reached one year of age. In 1907 the Borough of St. Pancras set up the first centre in the country at which mothers could get advice about bringing up their children. Within four years, about 100 similar centres had been opened in various parts of the country. In 1914 local councils were given government grants to open such centres. By that time, too, the majority of mothers could read and hundreds of pamphlets and small booklets were produced instructing them how to bring up their children correctly. By 1920, the child death rate had fallen to 80 per 1,000 births; in 1938, it was 53; and now it is about 20 per 1,000. The problem of just keeping children alive—which had baffled all previous generations—has been finally solved.

But at the beginning of the modern period deaths amongst young children were still rising. The cause of this was the introduction of elementary education for all. Before 1870 only two-fifths of working-class children aged from six to 10 went to school. By the 1880s, all children had to go, from the ages of five to 10 at least. Formerly, many of the very poorest children had not gone to school at all. Now, they were all crowded together in the same classrooms and the poorest children passed on to the others the diseases to which their living conditions made them so subject.

The health of some of these children was extremely poor. Some of them had tuberculosis. The poor conditions in which they lived made them easy victims of diphtheria, scarlet fever and dysentery. A large number of children—as many as one-third in the poorer areas of large cities—had rickets. Others had bad eyesight, decayed teeth or poor hearing.

What was needed was doctors in the schools themselves. In 1890, the London School Board appointed the first School Medical Officer in the country—Sir W. R. Smith. Three years later, the city of Bradford, one of the pioneers in this field, appointed the second school doctor—Dr. James Kerr. In 1907, it was made compulsory for all education authorities to employ school doctors. The size and scope of the service has increased so greatly that in 1957, Bradford, for example, was employing 40 whole-time officers and 13 part-time officers in its school medical service.

One of the basic causes of the children's bad health was lack of food. A survey carried out in 1904 showed that at least one-third of the pupils in elementary schools went hungry. They went to school having had no breakfast and went home again to not much more—a slice of bread and jam and a cup of tea without milk. It was not until all children were forced to go to school that the widespread extent of this starvation diet was revealed. Town officials, churchmen and many other middle-class people were so shocked that they set up organisations to feed the children.

In Bradford, for example, a Cinderella Club was formed in 1892 to provide free school dinners for poor children during the winter. The club was allowed to use the school cellars, free of charge, for preparing and serving the meals. Later on, a Mayor's Fund was opened to help provide money for school dinners.

The meals the Cinderella Club served may not now seem very appetising. In 1905 the menu was soup, bread and rice pudding on Monday, Wednesday and Friday, and hash, bread and rice pudding on Tuesdays and Thursdays. But these meals were much better than many of the children would have had at home. By 1905 there were about 200 organisations like the Cinderella Club in other big cities throughout the country and another 150 in London. In the following year, local authorities were allowed to pay for school dinners out of the rates. School dinners gradually improved. Some cities, like Bradford, started to serve school breakfasts, too. This continued from 1908 to 1932.

Some schoolchildren were neatly dressed, but often wore the same old patched clothes day after day without ever taking them off. A 1900 inquiry in one northern town showed that more than 100 schoolchildren had not taken off their clothes for six, seven or even eight months. It was the same in many other large towns and cities and in the country areas, too. In the villages of southern England in the 1890s—according to one writer— 'many big boys and girls are never made to change their day clothes to night ones till they go to service'. For this reason many of the children were infested with vermin. The same writer recommended mothers 'to crop the heads of little girls as well as boys till they leave school, as they can then be so easily washed and kept free from parasites'.

Not all of the village mothers followed this advice; in fact, some of them made a special effort to dress their little girls in pretty clothes. They were able to do so because the increasing production of cotton had made dress materials much cheaper.

But the same writer did not entirely approve of this new fashion of dressing up little village girls. 'Everyone, or nearly everyone, thinks that they *must have* things that are not only not necessary, but very unsuitable too.' It was wrong to make a tiny child wear gloves—particularly in the summer—and for the little girls at the village schools to have their hats covered with feathers or flowers instead of 'a sensible piece of ribbon' as was done 30 years before. With no nurses to run after them, the children looked like 'a dressed up doll (or monkey?) one minute, and the next not fit to be seen. . . . The most really important things in a girl's dress are boots and stays.' The stays, or corsets, should not be too stiff; and the boots, or shoes, should be nearly straight with low heels and fairly broad toes.

Until the most recent times very few children had many toys of their own. They were far too expensive for most people. A jigsaw puzzle for example, in 1815, cost about 13s. —a farm labourer's whole wages for a fortnight. If children had any toys at all they had probably been given to them, like the box of toys, a knife and fork, and two small chairs given to the little eight-year-old watercress seller described by Henry Mayhew in the middle of the nineteenth century. Otherwise, their toys were made out of natural objects—a doll, for example, from a ham bone. But most children, and particularly the poor, had only living dolls to play with. As the watercress seller said: 'I never had no doll; but I misses little sister—she's only two years old.'

It was not until 1850 that toys began to be manufactured on any large scale, but even then they remained too expensive for most parents to buy. Indeed, right up to the last war, there were very many children whose parents were too poor to buy them a pedal car or a tricycle and so the children made their own out of an orange box, four old wheels and other items of industrial scrap.

Games, however, needed little or no equipment, and had always been popular. For many years children had been playing the traditional games such as hide and seek (also called Hoop and Hide and Harry racket), leap-frog and blind man's bluff. Marbles were played with round stones or dried nuts, and in the country during the hop season, a hop-stem, stripped of its leaves, was used as a skipping rope. Rhyming games were also popular. In one of them the children chanted, 'Here comes my father all down the hill, all down the hill,' etc., to which the response was, 'We won't get up for his ugly face.' The refrains were then repeated, using the names of all the other members of the family, until they came to, 'Here comes my lover' to which the response was, 'We *will* get up for his lovely face.'

When children were not at school or were not doing some part-time job, these games were still one of their main forms of entertainment. Octavia Hill, who did so much in the second half of the nineteenth century to improve the living conditions of the people in London's slums, also tried to organise more games for their children. She introduced them to skipping, swinging and games with a bat and ball. Later she started drill for the boys and a drum and fife band, though she had difficulties in finding a sufficient number of 'ladies' to supervise these activities.

But these difficulties were to be overcome by an obscure secretary of a Sunday school mission in Glasgow—William Alexander Smith, who was later knighted. Like many other Sunday schoolteachers he was faced with the problem of retaining the interest of the older boys. On October 4, 1883, at the North Woodside Hall, Glasgow, he formed a group of some 30 boys called the Boys' Brigade. The main purpose was to teach religion through the Bible Class and discip-

Albion Street School, London.
1908.
The botany lesson.

line through drill. After a year, a uniform was introduced of a pill-box cap, and a white belt and haversack worn over the boys' ordinary clothes. Soon, a drum and fife band was added, too. The brigade was so successful that within three years there were 61 other companies with 2,000 members, mainly in Scotland. By the turn of the century, the Boys' Brigade had 20,000 members. There are now nearly 150,000 boys in the Brigade in Britain and another 70,000 overseas.

In 1908, Lt.-Gen. Baden-Powell started another uniformed organisation, the Scouts, whose membership was to increase so greatly that there are now nearly 7 million members in over 100 different countries. Both organisations had their critics. Nevertheless, they did a great deal, particularly in the early days, in getting children away from the towns into the countryside that they might otherwise have never seen, and in providing some central interests for their leisure time. The Boys' Brigade was one of the pioneers of camping; the first camp was held in 1886.

At the beginning of the present century there was a fairly complete system of elementary education with about 20,000 schools.

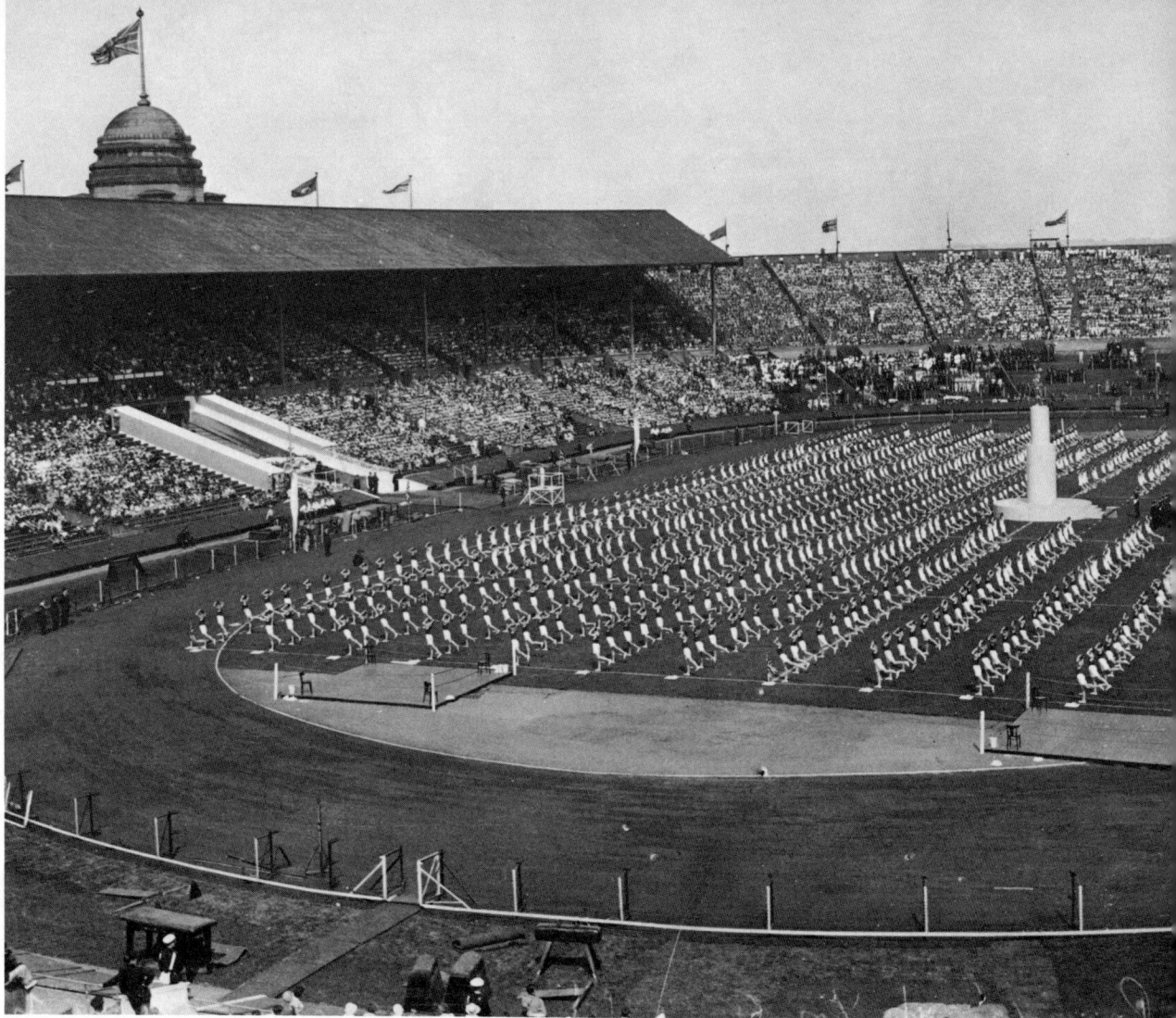

Nearly three-quarters of these were run by religious and voluntary bodies, while the remaining quarter were run by the School Boards set up under the 1870 Education Act. But most children still had only an elementary education, which lasted a few years. In 1893, the minimum age at which children could leave school was raised from 10 to 11; in 1899, it went up to 12; and in 1900 local authorities were given powers to raise it to 14.

Only about half of all the local authorities used these powers, and even those who did allowed many exemptions between the age of 12 and 14, particularly in Lancashire.

Two out of every five children still left school before reaching the age of 14. It was not until 1918 that it was made compulsory for children to stay at school until they were 14 and on April 1, 1947, the age was raised to 15.

Initially there were very few chances of ordinary children getting anything but an elementary education. In 1895, it was estimated that only four or five out of every thousand children went on from an elementary school to a grammar school. But from 1907, 'free places' were provided at the grammar schools and the new secondary schools for a few brighter pupils. After the

15

1.—SERVING OUT THE TEA.   2.—SELECTING CANDIDATES FOR ADMISSION INTO THE HOMES.   3.—WAIFS FOR THE DOCTOR'S CARE.
4.—"TWO ORANGES AND TWOPENCE ON GOING OUT!"
DR. BARNARDO'S FESTIVAL TO HOMELESS CHILDREN.

Dr. Barnardo's annual festival to
Homeless Children.
*In modern times homeless waifs
began to receive some
sympathetic care.*

First World War, State scholarships were introduced to allow poorer children to go to a university. From 1918, it was possible for some children to go each year from an elementary school to a secondary school by means of a 'free place' and then for 200 of the best pupils to go on to a university with a State scholarship. It was not until after the Second World War, when the 1944 Education Act came into effect, that secondary education was provided for all children. At the same time, grants from local authorities allowed more and more children to go on to some form of higher education. The opportunities for higher education are now expanding at an ever-increasing pace.

In the modern period a number of organisations have been set up to help children who were neglected or ill-treated by their parents. One of the first was formed by Dr. Thomas Barnardo, who opened a home for destitute children in Stepney Causeway in 1870. He then took over the Edinburgh Castle, a former gin palace, and turned it into a coffee palace, with a free medical mission and other social activities. The Salvation Army and the National Society for the Prevention of Cruelty to Children (NSPCC) are two other organisations which have worked prominently in this sphere. It was in 1883 that a Liverpool Society for the Prevention of Cruelty to Children was founded by T. F. Agnew, after visiting a similar society in New York. A London society was founded in the following year and five years later there were 31 committees throughout the country and the present national society was formed. In the provision of education, good medical services, school meals and care for neglected children, the State now does more for children than it has ever done before.

In the last 250 years, and particularly in the last 50, there has been a complete revolution in education and the attitude towards children. Two hundred years ago children were expected to work from an early age at some domestic industry or in the fields or, as the population of the industrial towns grew, in dark, insanitary factories. Education was still provided mainly by the dame's school or the charity school. Even so, the education they received was rudimentary and many children received none at all.

Now, every child must go to school until the age of 15 and, soon, until the age of 16. There are increasing opportunities for them to continue their education beyond those ages and many children wish to do so. Although some schools are old and overcrowded, many more are new and well equipped. There is an efficient medical service and a school meals service. Teachers have a much longer and more thorough training than they ever did in the past and there is a constant search to find improved methods of instruction and education. There are still many serious shortages and difficulties in all branches of education, but it is a measure of the changed attitudes towards education that these now cause such widespread public concern—not least among the teaching profession itself.

Summer Camp 1888.
Leisure activities for children began to be organised in the nineteenth century.

Modern Times and modern Pram.
Father takes over the care of baby, and trains it to appreciate the finer points of tennis.

A FLEET WEDDING.

Between a brisk young Sailor & his Landlady's Daughter at Rederiff.

Scarce had the Coach discharg'd its trusty Fare,	Pray step this way;—just to the Pen in Hand	Th'alarmed Parsons quickly hear the Din,	Till slow advancing from the Coaches Side,
But gaping Crowds surround th'amorous Pair:	The Doctor's ready there at your Command;	And haste with soothing Words t'invite 'em in:	Th' experienc'd Matron came (an artful Guide)
The busy Flyers make a mighty Stir!	This way (another cries) Sir I declare	In this Confusion jostled to and fro,	She led the way without regarding either,
And whispering cry, d'ye want the Parson, Sir?	The true and ancient Register is here:	Th'inamour'd Couple know not where to go;	And the first Parson spliced 'em both together.

WEDDING IN THE FLEET. (*From a Print of the Eighteenth Century.*)

A Fleet Wedding.
*An eighteenth century print
showing a sailor and his
landlady's daughter arriving for
their wedding.*

18

2. LOVE AND MARRIAGE

The Georgian Age

During the first half of the eighteenth century it was legal for a couple to get married in a tavern, a coffee house, a barber's shop, in one area of London. These *irregular marriages* took place around Fleet Prison. The first recorded marriage there in 1613 had been a perfectly proper ceremony conducted by the prison chaplain in the prison chapel. But as time passed, more and more people who wanted to get married in a hurry went to the Fleet Prison for the ceremony. No banns had to be read in church or a licence obtained. Many of the marriages were of young men who had run away with wealthy heiresses. At that time, a husband had complete control of his wife's money so that he wanted to get married quickly before the bride's parents could arrive to stop the ceremony. Others were between the adventuresses who used to loiter in Fleet Street and on Ludgate Hill hoping to trap some rich drunken man into marrying them. They never lived with their husband, but when he died they could claim his fortune as the legal wife. Other marriages were between ordinary couples, such as sailors home from the seas, who met a girl they fancied and, perhaps after knowing her for only a few days or a week, decided that they would like to wed.

Irregular marriages in the prison itself were stopped at the beginning of the eighteenth century, but other 'wedding shops' as they were called were soon opened in the neighbourhood. 'Chapels' were set up in taverns and gin palaces. Two of the best known were in a barber's shop called the Hand and Pen and in the Rainbow Coffee House. Most of the shops had a sign outside showing the clasped hands of a man and a woman and a notice underneath—Marriages Performed Within. Around the middle of the century, a clergyman, or an impostor dressed up in a cassock and gown to look like one, would marry any couple for a few shillings or 'a dram of gin or a roll of tobacco'—and no questions asked. Many of them married 2,000 or more couples a year. It was a lucrative trade. Some of the Fleet parsons became wealthy men, like Walter Wyatt who made nearly £700 in the year 1748 alone. The most notorious, and one of the wealthiest, was the Rev. Alexander Keith, of Mayfair Chapel, who once married the Duke of Hamilton to 'the youngest of the beautiful Miss Gunnings with a ring of the bed curtains at half-an-hour past twelve at night'.

Although these irregular marriages were legal, forcing wealthy widows or heiresses to marry against their will was not. It was common for newspapers of the time to have notices such as the following for

> apprehending David Power, and 16 other Persons concern'd in forcibly carrying away Henora Matthew, a Widow, and forcing her to marry the said David Power; and in order to deter others from such Practices, a Reward of £100 is offer'd for apprehending him, £20 a-piece for taking Milo Power his Brother, and the Priest that married them, and £5 each for the other Persons.

Fleet marriages were made illegal by Lord Hardwicke's Marriage Act of 1753. After the Act came into force the following year, marriages had to take place in church and banns had to be read for three successive Sundays or an expensive licence had to be obtained. Jews, however, were allowed to be married by their Rabbi and the Quakers in their meeting houses.

There were many critics of the new law. Some like the Rev. Alexander Keith said in a pamphlet that it would make marriage much more expensive. 'I have often heard a Flete-parson say, that many have come to be married when they have had but half-a-crown in their pockets and six-pence to buy a pot of beer. . . . Marriage in the method prescribed by the Act will come to six or eight times the sum.' Although he had an axe to grind, there were many other critics, too. Some said that the Act would restrict people's liberty and Horace Walpole described the reading of banns in church as an 'impudent ceremony'.

Engraved by W.T.Fry.

PHILIP YORKE, EARL OF HARDWICKE.

OB. 1764.

FROM THE ORIGINAL OF RAMSAY, IN THE COLLECTION OF

THE RIGHT HON^{ble} THE EARL OF HARDWICKE.

Lord Hardwicke.
*His Act stopped irregular
marriages in England.*

Honeymoon—Third Class.
Train travel allowed ordinary people to go to the seaside for their honeymoon.

There was still one loophole for runaway lovers. The Act did not apply to Scotland, where a couple could still get married legally by taking an oath in front of witnesses. The favourite spot for these marriages was Gretna Green, the first village over the border. The most famous Gretna Green 'parson' was Joseph Paisley, who held the office for 60 years from 1753 to 1813. He was not a blacksmith, as is commonly believed, but got that name through his quickness in forging the bonds between eloping couples; he had been a farmer originally, and then a fisherman. When he retired he was succeeded by Robert Elliott, who was married to Paisley's granddaughter. Elliott held the office for 29 years and claimed to have married more than 3,000 couples in that time.

Marriage then was much less of a formal ceremony than it is today. Some of the rich had elaborate church weddings, with the bride being preceded to the church by some boys wearing bride laces (broad ribbon tied about their silken sleeves). The bride might wear white, or silver—often a gown of brocaded satin or silk, a white hat and white, silk-fringed slippers.

Weddings could only be held between 8 a.m. and noon, so that the ceremony was followed by a wedding breakfast and sometimes by other festivities which lasted two or three days. Afterwards the couple might go off on their wedding tour, accompanied by one of the bridesmaids. To save this expense, some of the rich, and many of the middle classes, had a quiet wedding with only a few relatives present—or none at all.

Rich fathers sometimes told their daughters whom they had to marry and locked them in their rooms until they agreed to do so. And the future husband was often chosen solely on account of the size of his fortune. 'Young ladies' were educated primarily for marriage. They were taught to sing and to dance and to play a musical instrument in the hope that these accomplishments would persuade some rich man to marry them. A fictional heroine of the times, Moll Flanders, who became destitute and was taken in by a 'gentlewoman', describes how she received all the same 'advantages of education' as the daughters.

> . . . the lady had masters to the house to teach her daughters to dance, and to speak French, and to write, and others to teach them music; and as I was always with them, I learned as fast as they . . . so that, in short, I learned to dance and speak French as well as any of them. I could not so readily come at playing the harpsichord or spinet, because I had no instrument of my own to practise on. . . . But as to dancing, they could hardly help my learning country dances, because they always wanted me to make up (an) even number. . . .

It was also customary, though not obligatory, for all girls to ask their parents for permission to marry. At that time, with the limited opportunities for female employment, many daughters of small farmers worked as maidservants in the towns. In a book of model letters, written in the middle of the eighteenth century, the novelist Samuel Richardson showed the kind of correspondence that might ensue between the daughter and her parents. The daughter's letter stated:

> *Honoured Father and Mother.*
> I think it is my Duty to acquaint you, that I am addressed to for a change of condition, by one Mr. John Tanner, who is a

Glazier, and lives in the Neighbourhood by us. He is a young man of a sober Character, and has been set up about two Years, has good Business for his Time, and is well beloved and spoken of by every one. . . .

In their letter of reply, the parents said that they lived too far away to attend the wedding but would 'do some little Matters, as far as we are able, towards Housekeeping'. The girl then wrote back, saying that she had got married and that her master and mistress had 'made a present of three guineas towards Housekeeping', which, with the £20 she had saved herself, would enable them to set up home.

The wedding would probably have been a simple one, with the girl wearing no special dress, but her ordinary gown of pink or blue. To adorn herself, she might have borrowed, for a small sum, the bride gear—a set of jewels which the churchwardens kept in the parish chest, which was often locked with three separate keys to prevent theft.

But mainly because of the expense, many ordinary people did not bother with a church ceremony at all. As Jonas Hanway, the social reformer, wrote in 1754: 'With respect to amours in low life, how few are there which can be kept secret, in cases of pregnancy? . . . The common people in London are not very nice, and in the country it is a common practice to come together first and if they *prove*, as they term it, then they marry. This is a law of honor, like a gamester's debt.' These trial marriages were perhaps even more common in Scotland and Wales. In Scotland, there was an old custom of 'handfasting' in which couples pledged themselves to a trial marriage for a year merely by clasping hands. And in Wales there were similar customs marked by the giving of a richly-carved wooden love spoon to the bride.

For all people, except for the very rich who could afford to have a special Act of Parliament passed, there was no divorce. The Church courts could give a poor woman who had been brutally treated by her husband permission to live apart from him, but there was no guarantee that he would go on supporting her. Those people who were not afraid of defying the Church laws or of being prosecuted for bigamy did marry again. But more often, couples just lived together. Poor men occasionally sold their wives. In the eighteenth century one newspaper recorded that in Coventry:

> The following affair was transacted. . . . A Woman, being tired of her Husband, and the Man weary of his Wife, the Woman consented to have a Rope fastened to her Neck, be led by it to the Market Cross, and there sold for the amazing sum of Half a Crown; the new Husband received his Purchase with the greatest Marks of Pleasure, she only lamenting that her new Master was so advanced in Years, he being upward of Threescore.

Illegitimate children were common amongst all classes of society. Amongst the upper classes they were more easily accepted, than they were amongst the lower classes, who were punished not only for their sins but even more because it meant another mouth for the parish to feed. In 1776, the poor law authorities in Gloucester ordered that mothers of 'base born children' who became chargeable to the parish should be whipped. Many mothers died in giving birth to children. It was for that reason that, although there was no divorce, men frequently married two or three times in their lives.

Marriage certificate— *Gretna Green style.*

The Years of Growth

At the beginning of the nineteenth century the Church of England had a greater control over marriage than it had ever had before. Irregular marriages had been abolished in England, though they still continued in Scotland; and Roman Catholics and Dissenters, as well as members of the established Church, had to be married by a Church of England clergyman if they wanted their marriage to be recognised as valid. But this was soon to change. In 1836 an Act was passed which allowed Catholics and Dissenters to be legally married in their own places of worship. At the same time, civil marriages were made legal, so that couples who wished to do so could be married by a registrar, as they can be today. These register office weddings were not at first very popular. In the year ended June 30, 1838, out of a total of 111,481 marriages in England and Wales, only 1,093 took place in the Superintendent Registrar's office.

In spite of these changes, the way in which the mass of people behaved did not alter greatly. In the new industrial towns and in the remoter parts of the country, some people still went on as they had done for ages with their trial marriages, and, sometimes, bigamy as there was still no divorce. It was in vain for clergymen to try—as one of them did in a pamphlet called the *Golden Wedding Ring* published in 1830—'to restore marriage to its primitive sanctity, purity and bliss by pointing out its connection with religion'.

Too many people were still living in insanitary conditions in one room to be much affected by Victorian middle-class prudery —when the legs of tables were covered and girls were rebuked for mentioning 'unmentionables', such as nightdresses, in the presence of a man. In 1834, one clergyman reported to the Poor Law Commissioners that out of 20 poor girls who came to him to be married, 19 were pregnant on their wedding day. Girls and women in the mill towns eked out their small wages by prostitution. For P. Gaskell, writing in the 1830s,

it was the 'almost entire extinction of sexual decency' which was 'one of the darkest stains upon the character of the manufacturing population'. But there had been no 'extinction'. The 'manufacturing population' were behaving very much as they had always done. It was simply that the new respectable middle classes were more conscious and more critical of their moral defects.

The occasional selling, or swopping of wives, still continued. The custom was not confined entirely to the poor, for in 1815 it was reported that a young well-dressed lady with a silk halter around her shoulders was offered for sale at Smithfield. The price asked for 80 guineas, but eventually she was bought by a horse dealer for 50 guineas plus the horse on which he was mounted.

The practice was more common—and prices lower—amongst the poor. In the same year a man sold his wife and child for £1. And even in the 1880s two workmen in the Black Country were reported to have swopped wives on the way home from the pub— without their neighbours being in any way shocked by the exchange. Although the practice was by no means common, the belief lingered on in many people's minds that it was quite legal to sell a wife, so long as she was delivered to her new 'husband' with a halter around the neck.

Around the middle of the century in Wales, particularly in Caernarvonshire, Anglesey and parts of Merionethshire, a form of trial marriage known as 'bundling' was still practised. One writer of the times, the Rev. Caleb Brown, said that the men rarely deserted women who had made them happy, and marriage usually followed. 'When the match is made, a few days previous to the wedding, the parents of the parties have what is called a "bidding", or meeting of their friends at their separate homes. Presents and goods of every description and money— sometimes as much as £20, £30, or £40— are collected and help to establish the young couple in life.'

As the century progressed, and increasing prosperity allowed a new group of respect-

Victorian Wedding.
*An early photograph taken at the
height of middle-class
prosperity.*

able working-class families to establish themselves, attitudes towards marriage changed. The boy and girl 'kept company' for a longer period and often tried to put some money aside so that they could have a better start in married life.

These factors applied even more strongly in the middle classes, where education and training lasted longer, and the man was expected to be able to support his wife in the manner to which she had been accustomed. One book of etiquette, published in 1875, recommended that 'at twenty-five, if established in life, or with a reasonable prospect of being able to support a family, a young man may think of marriage, more especially if, in the society of his friends, he finds some person of suitable age, position and attraction'. The average age of marriage at that time was 26 for men and 24 for women.

The same book of etiquette also had some advice for girls who were thinking of marriage. 'Women in this matter (of marriage) have no choice but that of accepting or rejecting offers made to them, but to compensate for this they have far greater powers of adaptation than men have. They can more easily conform themselves to circumstances and to the character of the husbands than the husband can adapt to his wife's. . . . Self-sacrifice is the truest womanly virtue. . . . Always receive your husband with smiles, leaving nothing undone to render home agreeable, and gratefully reciprocate his kindness and attention. Study to gratify his inclinations in regard to food and cookery, in the management of the household, in your dress, manners and deportment. Never attempt to rule, or appear to rule, your husband. . . . If a lady understands that her duties are obedience, complaisance, an entire surrender of her will to that of her husband, and attention to his happiness as the first consideration, she has the spirit of the religious and civil idea of marriage.'

Even in the middle class, however, where girls were trained from an early age to accept an inferior status, it was not always possible for them to sustain these remarkable qualities of self-sacrifice. In spite of the long engagements, life was so formal that couples often did not really get to know each other well until they were married. Both the young man and the girl were on their best behaviour while they were engaged. Then followed all the excitement of preparing for the wedding, the great day itself, and finally the honeymoon, or wedding tour, as it was still often called at that time. By the middle of the nineteenth century it was customary for the couple to go off on their honeymoon alone without any one of the bridesmaids accompanying them. The couple might have gone to Cornwall, Devon, the Lake District, North Wales, or the lakes of Killarney, which were all favourite honeymoon spots. Richer couples went abroad—to France, Germany or Switzerland.

But if the marriage did not work out, there was no divorce. Marriage then lasted literally 'until death us do part'. Divorce was still only for the very wealthy. A Royal Commission on Divorce in 1850 estimated that the total cost of an absolute divorce at that time was about £700 or £800, and if a great amount of litigation was involved it could be very much higher. Divorce could still only be obtained by special Act of Parliament. In the two centuries from 1650 to 1850 there were only 300 divorces in all. To make divorce easier and cheaper a Matrimonial Causes Act was passed in 1857 which set up the divorce court. The Act made it very much easier for a man to get a divorce. He had to prove only that his wife had been unfaithful, while the wife had to show that her husband had not only been unfaithful but had also been cruel or had deserted her.

Even after the Act was passed, very few people took advantage of it. For the next 30 years the average number of divorce cases was only about 140 a year. Although a divorce could now be obtained legally, the majority of middle-class people still considered that it was not respectable. It was considered better that couples should suffer their quarrels in private rather than publicly avow their differences. For men, divorce often meant the end of their public careers; for women, it meant that they could no longer be accepted by polite society. In 1886, a politician, Charles Wentworth Dilke, was forced to retire from public life after being cited in a divorce case; and four years later another politician, Charles Stewart Parnell, had his career wrecked for the same reason.

Although divorce had been made cheaper, it was still far too expensive for the working class. Among the very poor, particularly, many husbands treated their wives with great brutality. Around the middle of the nineteenth century, the Rev. J. Shearman, a domestic missionary in Bristol, reported that 'parentage commences early in life. . . . An infant is born; the bed upon the floor, and made up of straw gathered from many places, with cloths of several forms and colours. I have seen a mother with a black eye, before her child was a month old. . . .'

It was not until 1878 that an act was passed giving magistrates' courts powers to grant a separation order with maintenance to wives who had been assaulted by their husbands. By the end of the century about 8,000 separation orders were being granted every year. In this way, wives could escape their husband's brutality, but because divorce was still too expensive for them, they could not hope to remarry legally. Many men and women broke the law by marrying again, even though they were not divorced. But sympathetic judges often gave a nominal sentence to these people who had committed bigamy. Individuals often act more humanely than the letter of the law.

Modern Times

Nearly 40 years ago—in 1931—only 25 per cent of women between the ages of 20 and 24 were married; now, well over half of the women in this age group are wives. Since the end of the last war there has also been a considerable increase in the number of teenage marriages. Although some people think it is unwise for couples to get married when they have only just left school, until recently it was possible for people to get married at an even earlier age. Until 1929, when the minimum age of marriage was raised to 16, it was possible for a boy to be married at 14 and a girl at 12—with their parents' consent. There were, however, very few of these child marriages. In the three years before 1929 the average number of marriages of people under 16 was only 45 a year. Of these, two were boys and 43 were girls.

Throughout the modern period, too, civil marriage has become more popular. At the beginning of the modern period, in 1884, only 13.1 per cent of marriages in England and Wales took place in a register office; in 1961 it had risen to nearly 30 per cent. Nevertheless, most couples still prefer to get married in a church or a chapel.

It is only in very recent times that people of all kinds have been prosperous enough to spend money freely on a wedding celebration. At the beginning of the modern period, even many of the middle classes were complaining about the needless expense of weddings. These middle-class weddings, however, were more elaborate than most weddings today. Because the Church would allow marriages to take place only between 8 a.m. and noon, the ceremony was followed, not by a reception, but by a wedding breakfast. This was an expensive, formal, sit-down meal, usually held at the bride's home, where large quantities of food and champagne, at 36s. for a dozen bottles, were consumed. In 1886, the Church extended the permitted hours of marriage from 8 a.m. to 3 p.m. People started to marry later in the day and the wedding breakfast began to go out of fashion. Instead, the wedding party went either to the bride's home, a hotel, or hired rooms, for a much less formal and less expensive reception. In 1934, the time during which marriage could take place was further extended to 6 p.m.

In 1886, when the hours of marriage were first extended, many working-class families still could not afford to have a very elaborate wedding. Even if they could not afford to have an organist playing in the church, they had music of a different kind outside. One writer said in 1888 that 'on the marriage of a journeyman butcher his companions treated him to a performance of the "marrow bones and cleaver"'. When the bride and groom left the church it was customary to throw rice at them. To save money, as one clergyman the Rev. R. Wilberforce Starr observed in 1898, 'of late, it has become customary among the humbler candidates for matrimony, to receive a shower of tiny coloured paper when leaving the church door. It is a poor innovation, however, and it is not likely to beat the old-fashioned rice out of the field.'

If the husband could not afford to buy a wedding ring, 'often the working girl—soon to be a bride—buys her own ring herself'. wrote the same clergyman. 'And no matter how poor or ragged she may be, the ring must be of undoubted quality.' The middle classes at that time favoured a thin ring, but the working classes, particularly in the north, wanted something that looked more substantial and costly, so that they more often chose a thick, broad ring. But then, unlike the middle classes, they very often had no engagement ring. For them, there was very often no formal engagement. 'The working classes,' one writer said at the beginning of this century, 'have at all times enjoyed a freedom from the rules of etiquette, as it is understood in the circles above them, and the process of natural selection has been usually followed.' They 'kept company' and married when they could afford to do so. They might have a short honeymoon at a seaside resort and would then return to start

their married life, usually in the parents' home or in rooms.

The man was still very much the 'boss' in his own home. When times were hard it was he who was given the best food. The children came next; while the mother often went without. The wife was expected to wait on her husband hand and foot. The husband might grow a few vegetables on an allotment, or in the garden if they had one, but he expected to do very little work in the house. Often his wife would not know what he was earning. He would give her the housekeeping money on which she had to manage somehow, by living on credit or by going to the pawnbroker. With the gradual increase in wages, men expected to keep enough money for betting, smoking, drinking and a Saturday afternoon visit to a football match.

Throughout most of the period, there was always a large number of women who could not get married even if they wanted to: there were just not enough men to go round. Until very recently there were always more boys who died at birth and in the first few years of life. Even though more boys than girls were born, so many of the boys died that there was a surplus of women between the marriageable ages of 20 and 50. At the beginning of the century there were about 107 women to every 100 men in this age range. Many of them would be 'left on the shelf', particularly once they had reached the age of 40. As the Rev. R. W. Starr wrote: 'There is a good demand for widows between the ages of 25 and 49; they are fairly popular at the latter age, whereas spinsters have little prospect of a wedding ring after the age of 39.'

This disparity in the number of men and women excluded many women from all hopes of having a home and children of their own and condemned them to a lonely, embittered life dreaming of the man who had somehow got away. Now, with the great decrease in the infantile death rate—so that more boys survive the first few testing years of life—this problem has virtually disappeared. It is not until the age of about 45

Bride and Sweep.
A pre-war custom: a kiss from a chimney sweep was thought to bring the bride good luck.

that the number of women starts to exceed the number of men.

Perhaps the greatest change in married life has been caused by family planning and birth control. This subject first received wide publicity in 1877 when Charles Bradlaugh and Mrs. Annie Besant were prosecuted for circulating a birth control pamphlet. It was not until after the First World War that birth control was more generally practised by all sections of the population. Much of this was due to the pioneering work of Dr. Marie Stopes, who was mainly responsible for a birth control clinic being opened in Holloway, London, in 1921. It moved to its present site in Whitefield Street in 1925.

The decline in the size of families has been dramatic. A century ago, women on average had six children; but couples who were married between 1934 and 1943 had, on average, only just over two. In the inter-war years when money was scarcer than it is now, even many young lower middle-class people made a deliberate choice whether they should have a child or a car—a choice

summed up in a phrase of that time 'a baby, or a baby Austin', which in the 1930s cost £125. In many families, too, birth control created a completely new kind of problem—that of the 'only child'.

In the post-war years there has been some change in the attitude towards marriage itself. More and more women continue working after they are married and this greater independence, plus a change in the attitude towards women, has meant that many younger people tend to look upon marriage as a partnership rather than a relationship in which the man is dominant. At the same time, higher wages for young people allow them to marry and to set up their own home at an increasingly early age. This has resulted in a considerable change from a three-tier or three-generation family unit consisting of grandparents, parents and children to a two-tier unit of parents and children alone.

Another major change has been in the attitude towards divorce. This started after the First World War as the following table shows:

NUMBER OF
DIVORCES GRANTED

1900	494
1913	870
1917	946
1921	3,936

Young men got married in haste before they went off to the war. When they returned some of them found that their wives had been unfaithful to them. Although they had married in haste, they no longer had to repent in leisure, for the divorce courts were open to all. If their savings or capital totalled less than £50, they could get most of the lawyer's fees and other legal expenses paid for them by the State, under the poor person's rules.

Women, too, had become more independent, running the family business single-handed while the men were away, working in munition factories, and doing all kinds of jobs that formerly had been done only by men. It was only just over a century since the first woman had obtained a divorce from her husband. Now more and more women started to do so. It was made much easier for them after 1923 when a law was passed which allowed a woman to divorce her husband just because he had been unfaithful to her. Women's claims for equality had triumphed as they were beginning to do in so many other spheres. By 1937 the number of successful divorce petitions had reached a total of over 5,000 a year. In that year, Sir Alan Herbert's Act was passed which allowed people to get a divorce for the first time on the grounds of cruelty, desertion or insanity alone. By 1939, there were over 8,000 successful petitions.

The Second World War, like the first, produced a great rise in the total number.

NUMBER OF
DIVORCES GRANTED

1939	8,248
1946	31,871
1947	52,249

The number of divorces granted in 1947 was an all-time record; after that the total started to decline again. But in the last few years it has started to go up again. One of the main reasons for this is that more and more teenagers are getting married, before some of them are really mature enough to do so.

There has also been a great alteration in the attitude towards divorce; few people, apart from Catholics, are entirely opposed to it. Because of this change of attitude and the greater ease of getting a divorce, there has been a great increase in the number of marriages that break up. Just before the First World War—in 1911—only 0·2 per cent of marriages in England and Wales ended in divorce, but by 1950 the percentage had risen to 7·1. Between 70 and 80 per cent of those who divorce get married again. This seems to indicate that the attitude towards marriage as an institution has not changed, only that people now have a greater opportunity to leave a partner they have chosen mistakenly.

There have been considerable changes in the form of marriage during the last 200 years and some in the nature of marriage itself. In the eighteenth century many ordinary people, particularly in the country districts, were never formally married in church, but simply went through a traditional ceremony, which to them was probably just as meaningful. There was no divorce, except for the very rich, but some people comitted bigamy by marrying again illegally or just lived with another person.

Lord Hardwicke's Marriage Act of 1753 abolished irregular weddings in England and made the only legal form of marriage (except for Jews and Quakers) one conducted by a Church of England clergyman. The act did not have very great effects upon ordinary people as most of them had very little property to leave when they died and were, therefore, not particularly concerned whether their marriage was recognised as valid or not. It was far more middle-class pressures which were responsible for the passing of a new law in 1836 which allowed Catholics and Dissenters to be married in their own churches and chapels and also instituted a civil form of ceremony in a register office. Divorce courts were set up in 1857, but it was not until after the First World War that divorces became at all common. Since then, the number of divorces has risen greatly.

In marriage and divorce there was been a somewhat circular pattern of change, so that couples can now do legally what they once had to do outside the law: the traditional ceremony has been replaced by an official register office wedding, and easier divorce has made it possible for more couples to remarry legally.

There have also been some changes in the nature of marriage itself, particularly in the decades since the end of the Second World War. More and more couples tend to look upon marriage as a partnership and increasing affluence has allowed couples to marry at an earlier age and to set up their own separate home more easily. The two-tier or two-generation family unit has increasingly replaced the three-generation, producing a new problem of old people who have to live alone. At the same time the birth rate has risen from its low point in the 1930s, so that the problem of the 'only' child is not so great as it once was.

A weaver's home.
Before the factory age, the home was often both a dwelling place and a workshop.

Woman Spinning.
An interior of a Yorkshire cottage at the beginning of the nineteenth century.

3. WORK AND LEISURE

The Georgian Age

Though the growing number of factories began to attract more people into the new industrial towns, most people throughout this whole period still lived in the country—in small towns and villages—just as they had always done. But the countryside itself was not exempt from change. The increasing enclosure of the waste land stopped farm workers in some areas from keeping a pig or chickens of their own, which could make a great difference to the family budgets of those days. There was also less work for their wives to do, particularly after Hargreaves invented his spinning jenny in 1765 and Cartwright his mechanical loom in 1787. These inventions made domestic spinning and weaving more and more unprofitable. Work was taken out of the cottages into the factories.

The population explosion of the eighteenth century increased the demand for food, causing prices to rise. At the same time, a series of bad harvests, particularly towards the end of the period, and the war with France, also helped to push up prices. In spite of these higher prices and more efficient farming methods, wages rose very little. On the whole, farm labourers were probably worse off at the end of the period than they were at the beginning.

Not that their lives had ever been very luxurious, or free. They were very much at the mercy of the weather: bad weather resulted not only in poor harvests and therefore higher prices, but also in less work. And they were dependent on the charity of the local gentry and the honesty of the parish overseer.

There was little they could do to escape the conditions into which they had been born. Travel was slow, difficult, dangerous and expensive—even for the rich. Around the middle of the eighteenth century, Scottish travellers often used to make out their wills before attempting the perilous journey to London, because of the ever-present dangers of highwaymen. Ordinary people, at that time, sometimes never left the village or town in which they had been born, except to visit the nearest fair or festival. Alexander Somerville, the son of a Scottish farm labourer, described in his autobiography the astonishment he felt when he went to a fair with his two sisters in 1820. He was about nine years of age at the time. 'I had never before seen a town, nor village, nor shops, nor a stall, nor a coin of any kind spent, nor an article of any description purchased. The fair consisted of about 100 head of cattle and perhaps 200 people, and as I had never seen such an assemblage before, I was amazed and we stood the great part of the day gazing at the riches of a stall of gingerbread. . . .'

To move permanently from your birthplace was sometimes to invite misfortune. For in doing so you would probably run the risk of having no relief in sickness or in unemployment in the new parish to which you moved. Nevertheless, many people took this chance, attracted by the higher wages in the new industrial towns. And in every age there have been those blessed with intelligence, ambition, courage, good looks, or just sheer luck, who have been able to escape from the conditions in which they had been born and to make a new and more prosperous life for themselves and their families. Alexander Somerville was just one example of this kind: born a farm labourer's son, he became a successful journalist and writer. There were many more like him, but they constituted only a minority and, on the whole, during this period, many people preferred to stay where they were in the country—and to stick it out.

The farm labourer's life was hard. When he was employed, his hours of work were long, often lasting from 6 a.m. to 9 p.m. And his wages were low—only 5s. a week, sometimes, in winter when work was scarce, rising to as much as 10s. a week at harvest time. The budget of one farm labourer in Barkham, Berkshire, in 1787, was as follows:

Weekly Expences of a Family, consisting of a Man and his Wife, and five Children, the eldest eight years of age, the youngest an Infant.

	s.	*d.*
FLOUR: 7½ gallons, at 10*d.* per gallon	6	3
Yeast, to make it into bread, 2½*d.*; and salt 1½*d.*	0	4
Bacon, 1 lb. boiled at two or three times with greens; the pot-liquor, with bread and potatoes, makes a mess for the children	0	8
Tea, 1 ounce, 2*d.*;—¾ lb. sugar, 6*d.*; —½ lb. butter or lard 4*d.*	1	0
Soap, ¼ lb. at 9*d.* per lb.	0	2¼
Candles, ⅓ lb. one week with another at a medium, at 9*d.*	0	3
Thread, thrum, and worsted, for mending apparel, etc.	0	3
Total	8	11¼

Weekly Earnings of the Man and his Wife, viz.

	s.	*d.*
The man receives the common weekly wages 8 months in the year	7	0
By task-work the remaining 4 months he earns something more: his extra earnings, if equally divided among the 52 weeks in the year, would increase the weekly wages about	1	0
The wife's common work is to bake bread for the family, to wash and mend ragged clothes, and to look after the children; but at bean-setting, haymaking, and harvest, she earns as much as comes one week with another to about . . .	0	6
Total	8	6

	s.	*d.*
Weekly expences of this family . .	8	11¼
Weekly earnings	8	6
Deficiency of earnings	0	5¼

This budget, and five others, were obtained by the Rector of Barkham, the Rev. David Davies. All the other budgets were very similar. Bacon was the basic meat in all families, though they sometimes had a sheep's head instead. Few of the families had more than 1 lb. of meat a week, and most of it was coarse and fat. The butter was usually rancid. To eke out their soap, some of the families burnt green fern and kneaded the ashes into balls, from which they made a solution for washing.

The Rev. Davies then asked vicars and other people in various parts of the country to send in six farm labourers' budgets from their own areas. Although there were variations in the prices of some goods—particularly of coal, cheese and meat—these other budgets showed that those from Barkham were fairly representative of the country as a whole.

Indeed, the farm labourers of Barkham were by no means the worst off. The Rev. Etterick reported from Aff-Piddle, Dorset, that 'many working men breakfast and dine on dry bread alone, without either cheese or drink of any kind; their meal is supper, and that generally is no better than unpeeled potatoes, and salt, or barley-cake fried, and water.' In Narton, Westmorland, where there was no local manufacturing industry at all, conditions were particularly bad. The farm labourers had no meat or bacon. Their bread was made of rye and barley. They lived almost entirely on bread and milk, porridge—which they called 'hasty pudding' —and potatoes.

In the first half of the eighteenth century, when prices were lower, most workers had had a different kind of diet—more meat and cheese, black bread made from rye or barley instead of white bread, and beer instead of tea. The poor were often criticised for eating white bread and for not eating more potatoes. But as the Rev. Davies pointed out, wheaten bread was the 'only good thing of which they can have sufficiency' and it 'may be eaten alone with pleasure; but potatoes require either meat or milk to make them go down:

you cannot make many hearty meals of them with salt and water only'.

Tea, which had first been used in England at the beginning of the eighteenth century, was drunk by the farm labourers not because they no longer liked beer, but because the latter had become so expensive. At the beginning of the century, most people still brewed their own beer. This *small beer*, which had a low alcohol content of only 2 to 3 per cent, was drunk at every meal. But a heavy tax on malt put home-brewed beer out of the reach of many people, though in some parts of the country it was still made. In other places, the farm labourer received a gallon of beer a day free of charge, but his wages were lower than the average, only 4s. 6d. a week. At harvest time the men might drink eight or ten quarts in a day.

At first, tea had been drunk only by the rich, but by about the middle of the eighteenth century it was being drunk by all social classes. In the more remote parts of the country, however, there were still some people who did not know what tea was. In a book published in 1745, Simon Mason tells how a 'country dame' was sent half a pound of tea as a present by her sister in London. 'My Dame was quite a Stranger to the Use of this new-fashioned genteel Herb, but thought it, like most other Herbs, good Eating with Bacon and accordingly tied it up in a Cloth, and boiled it. She boiled it above two Hours, till she had almost spoiled her Bacon, then took it up, and as a great Rarity, melted some Butter and Vinegar to it. My Dame with her good Man and the rest of her Household, sat down to Dinner; upon chewing this Sallad they found it very tough.'

At that time there was still a great deal of opposition to tea-drinking, not so much on medical grounds (though its effects on health were disputed) as for social reasons. The same writer observed that afternoon tea-drinking 'especially among the lower sort, has impoverished many families; not from the Expence altogether, but by idle gossiping Meetings, which abound with Scandal,

His Majesty's Bear-Garden.
Eighteenth century announcement of a duel, with boxing displays as usual.

Reproach, Backbiting, and ill Advice. . . .' Nevertheless, the drinking of tea increased enormously. The poor drunk the cheaper sort—brown not green—and sweetened it with cheap brown sugar. They drank their tea weak and without milk. In many parts of the country, and particularly near London, milk was almost unobtainable by the poor; it was all sent to London or used to rear calves which could be sold to rich people for veal.

Even if a farm labourer's family had a small surplus on its weekly budget—as some of them had—this was in most cases turned into a deficit by the necessary annual expenses. Davies calculated these as 2s. 8¼d. a week. Rent of a cottage, or part of a vacated farmhouse, came to between £2 and £2 2s. a year. Often a small patch of garden went with the house, where the labourer might grow a few herbs and fresh vegetables to supplement his meagre diet. Some of them were lucky enough to have grazing rights on the common or waste and were able to keep a pig or a few chickens. But in Barkham the farmers refused to grant these rights to those who had been moved into part of an old farmhouse, vacated when a farm was enclosed or sold up.

In some parts of the country, the cottages were built of brick or stone and had glazed windows, but more often, according to contemporary writers, they were built of wood or of mud mixed with straw. Often they had only one room for the whole family to live and sleep in. The window space was sometimes covered with scraps of rags to keep out the cold and rain. Those few families who were fortunate enough to possess a window of their own carried it from house to house when they moved and fixed it in the window space of their new home. The floor was usually mud, beaten down into a cold damp mess by the passing feet of the family. There was often scarcely any furniture—perhaps a few wooden or rush-seated chairs, a table—sometimes made of rough planks nailed together—and in some houses, though not in all, a bed.

As a child, Alexander Somerville lived with his mother and father and his seven brothers and sisters in a shabby-looking tiled shed in Springfield, Scotland. It was about 12 feet by 14 feet and was 'too low to allow a man to stand upright. . . . Without ceiling, or anything beneath the bare tiles of the roof; without a floor save the common clay; without a cupboard or a recess of any kind; with no grate but the iron bars which the tenants carried to it, built up, and took away when they left it; with no partition of any kind save what the beds made; with no window save four small panes on one side. . . .'

Many cottages had no other means of cooking than the open fire, but some cottages, including those in Barkham, had ovens of their own. Turf cut from the common was often used as fuel. A load, sufficient for the whole year, cost 12s. But as it took only about a week to cut and collect it, most farm labourers in Barkham did the work themselves, borrowing a cart from a farmer to carry it back home. In some favoured parts of the country there was ample wood or peat to use as fuel, but in other places, people had to be content with gorse or furze or balls of dried cow dung. The cottage was lit either by candles, which were heavily taxed, or by rush-lights, made at home from dried rushes dipped in bacon fat.

One of the biggest items in the farm labourer's budget was clothing. It cost about £3 10s. 0d. a year to clothe a family, though most people could not afford to spend that much, unless the wife could work to supplement the family income. The annual expenditure for a man was given by the Rev. David Davies as: wear of a suit per year, 5s.; working jacket and breeches, 4s.; two shirts, 8s.; one pair of stout shoes nailed, 7s.; two pairs of stockings, 4s.; hat, handkerchief etc., 2s. The expenditure for a woman was: wear of gown and petticoats, 4s.; one shift, 3s. 6d.; one pair of strong shoes, 4s.; one pair of stockings, 1s. 6d.; two aprons, 3s.; handkerchiefs, caps etc., 4s. Usually, the children's clothes were 'partly made up of the parents' old clothes, partly bought at second hand'.

Most of their clothes were made of heavy wool or linen, which was difficult to wash and keep clean. The man's breeches were often made of leather. He wore a handkerchief round his neck. The wife's stockings were frequently made of black worsted. Her apron was white and her shoes black. In some parts of the country, labourers wore clogs.

In addition to these expenses, there was also the cost of lying-in, which occurred on average every two years, and the cost of 'physick' in sickness and of burial—mothers nearly always lost at least one child. All the six families investigated by Davies had an annual deficiency in their budgets. The deficit had to be made up by poor relief from the parish. Out of 200 residents, one-fifth were receiving relief, either individually or in the poorhouse.

The Elizabethan Poor Laws, amended though they were, had never been designed to cope with mass unemployment. What was sorely needed was an increase in wages, and indeed in 1795 a Bill was introduced into the House of Common to secure a minimum wage—a measure far in advance of the general attitudes of those times. It was defeated. Instead, in the same year, the magistrates of Speen, in Berkshire, decided to make up the difference between the labourer's wage and the cost of living—determined then solely by the price of bread—through subsidies from the poor rates. This system of outdoor relief was used instead of sending people to the poorhouse. It had already been operating in some parts of the country for a number of years; but the 'Speenhamland system' was adopted so widely that it governed the operation of the poor law for the next 40 years.

There were many critics of this system of outdoor relief. Davies said that it did not always go to those who deserved it most; many overseers were corrupt; and it was 'a great discouragement to the industrious poor'. And William Belsham, writing in 1797, said: 'The relief of large numbers exceeds the limits of private ability. . . . A nation is not to relieve the distresses of the Poor by Acts of charity; it ought to prevent their existence by acts of justice.' These two voices represented a small, but significant, minority of people who even then believed that greater social justice was the answer to the nation's ills.

Life for the country poor, however, was not entirely lacking in entertainment. Because there was little else for them to do, they went to the alehouse, where beer cost 1d. a pot and a pipe could be borrowed for a returnable $\frac{1}{2}d$. deposit. It was, there, too, that country-people planned their poaching expeditions. Poaching was very common, even though some estates were protected by man-

traps and spring guns, and magistrates could sentence poachers to transportation to the colonies for life.

Drinking was particularly heavy at the week-ends. In 1810, Hannah More said that many men preferred to drink water all the week so that they could get really drunk once a week. Most farm labourers were paid late on Saturday night. As a consequence, the Rev. Davies said, a large part of their wages were squandered away in the alehouse on Sunday, while the wife and children were, in his picturesque phrase, 'abandoned to hunger and nakedness'. Another consequence was that many of them never went to the Sunday service, even though they could be fined for not doing so. But it was also 'the meanness of dress' that made 'many of the poor ashamed to appear among decent people at our services'.

It is difficult to know what religion really meant to these people. Christian baptism and burial were important to them, though it is difficult to say whether it was through true belief, social convention, or superstition. It seems doubtful if there was as much fervour in their feeling towards the Church of England as there was, say, towards the Primitive Methodists. This branch of the Methodist Church was founded by William Clowes of Burslem and Hugh Bourne of Stoke-on-Trent in 1805. Though it never had many adherents, it was almost entirely run and attended by the working classes.

There was also much drinking on feast days, such as May Day and Harvest Home. These occasions were often also marked by fairs and festivals—at which there were many entertainments, some of them brutal and associated with gambling. There was bear-baiting and bull-baiting, in which the bull was tethered to a stake by a rope and then baited by dogs. Cock-fighting was another popular diversion. A variation on this was throwing sticks at cockerels to see who could kill the bird first. It was also the age of the prize fight with bare hands. The fights lasted for hours and sometimes ended with disappointed gamblers invading the ring

The Cockfight.
*Hogarth's impression of this
popular eighteenth century sport
for all classes.*

to take their own revenge with sticks and whips upon the victor. Wrestling matches were common, too. There were also gentler amusements, such as quoits—played in the country with a horseshoe—ninepins, shovel-board, sack races, running and jumping contests, and catching a pig with a greased tail.

Cricket and football had originally been country sports, but both were to be organised and taken over by the gentry. Cricket was first played by shepherds with their crooks, using the wicket gate as a target for the bowlers. But in the eighteenth century the game became fashionable amongst the rich. The first 'county' match was played be-

tween the Londoners and Kent in 1719, and in 1744 the first match whose whole score still survives was played at the Artillery Ground, Finsbury, between Kent and All England. In 1787, the MCC (Marylebone Cricket Club) was formed; it has retained its control over the rules of the game to this day.

Football had originally been a sport played between opposing teams in the village street with great rowdiness and much violence. During the eighteenth century it gradually died out, except in a few places where it was still played at Shrovetide. By about the beginning of the nineteenth century it had almost entirely ceased; but it was to be revived later in the century at the public schools.

In most country districts the highlight of the year was the celebration of public events, such as great victories, coronations, and royal births, marriages and jubilees. The church bells pealed, debtors were freed from prison, services were held, and the poor had the rare treat of tasting the traditional fare of old England—roast beef—and plum pudding, washed down with liberal amounts of free ale.

To commemorate the 49th anniversary of George III on October 25, 1809, there were widespread celebrations. In Petersham, Surrey, all 70 children of the parish were 'completely clothed in such colours as their parents desired'; while at Rugeley, Staffordshire, feasts were held for the poor followed by 'a dance in the open air, where high and low, rich and poor, intermixed with each other'. Similar celebrations were held elsewhere. They were paid for by the local gentry. At Devizes, Wiltshire, one of the sponsors was 'Miss Beffin, the celebrated Lady without arms and legs, who . . . gave an ox to be roasted whole on the green'.

Not all of the country-people were in quite so desperate a position as the farm labourers. There were still many small farmers—particularly in the north—who were slightly better off. There was also a remarkable variety of craftsmen of all kinds, including apothecaries, chandlers, clockmakers, joiners, saddlers, stone cutters and whitesmiths, who lived at a somewhat higher standard than did the farm labourers. To enter some of these trades as an apprentice, a premium of £40 to £50 was often demanded, which was quite beyond the means of most farm labourers, though within the reach of other craftsmen, artisans and small tradesmen. Entry into the most prosperous businesses was completely out of the reach of any of these people; a 'gentleman of respectability' advertising in *The Times* towards the end of the period offered £1,000 for 'an adequate mercantile situation'.

For the poor, there were on the whole bigger opportunities in the large cities and the capital than there were in the country. At the same time, there were greater depths of degradation into which the unsuccessful could sink. At the time when farm labourers

An early cricket match
It took place at Brading in the middle of the eighteenth century.

39

were commonly earning 6s. or 7s. a week, a Witney blanket weaver was earning 11s. and a Durham miner or keelman 14s. a week— plus abundant supplies of coal. There were in the towns just as great dangers of un- employment and perhaps less certainty of poor relief. Town housing was in some ways even worse than it was in the country: the working class lived mainly in tenements opening on to sordid, sunless courts—parti- cularly in London. Few working people, even craftsmen and skilled labourers, occu- pied more than one or two rooms and the poorest lived huddled together in one small room in a cellar, unventilated except by a wooden flap, and subject to flooding. This room was often, for the cobbler or the second- hand clothes dealer, his place of business as well as his home.

Even so, there were significant differences in the way the London workers and the farm labourers lived. As the one-room homes of the London poor were often devoid of all means of cooking, they took to buying ready- cooked meats and pies from shops. In the first half of the eighteenth century, coach- men and draymen might eat their midday meal of tripe, cowheel or shin of beef in a cellar 'dive'.

They also tended to take up the sophisti- cated tastes of the rich quicker than country- folk did. Tea-drinking had become fashion- able amongst working people in London when it was still scarcely known at all in some parts of the country. The clothes they wore were most often second-hand and some- times as patched and ragged as those worn by the labouring poor in the country—but they were at least more fashionable. There was an enormous trade in second-hand clothes. Some were supplied by servants, who had a right to their master's or mistress's dis- carded clothing, and some were stolen.

The London poor preferred to drink gin rather than beer. Between 1700 and 1735 the consumption of gin was estimated to have increased over ten times. By the middle of the eighteenth century, every fourth or fifth house in some of the slum areas of London, such as St. Giles, sold gin. The effects of this injurious liquor were so harmful that in 1751 the duty on gin was raised substantially. This increase, combined with a rise in the price of grain, had trebled the price of gin by 1758, but many people still went on drinking it. Towards the end of the period a number of tracts were published, condemning the evils of gin-drinking. Some of them, like the following, were in verse:

Look through the Land from North to
    South
And look from East to West;
And see what is to Englishmen,
Of Life the deadliest Pest.

It is not Want, tho' that is bad
Nor War, tho' that is worse;
But Britons brave endure, alas!
A self-inflicted Curse.

Go where you will throughout the Realm
You'll find the reigning Sin,
In Cities, Villages and Towns;
The Monster's name is GIN.

The State compels no man to drink
Compels no man to game;
'Tis GIN and gambling sink him down
To rags, and want, and shame. . . .

Although the differences in wealth be- tween the rich and the poor were enormous the gap between them in some ways was less than it was to become in the Victorian age. The interests—and even the attitudes—of the rich and poor were similar. Some gentle- men were just as interested in cock-fighting, pugilism, gambling and drinking as were the poor. Their greater wealth simply enabled them to indulge on a grander scale. Charles James Fox lost £140,000 at gambling before he was 25, and the rich commonly drank three or four bottles of port in an evening— apart from what they had had during the rest of the day.

Ladies' cricket match.
*Played between the Ladies of
Rochester and the Ladies of
Maidstone in 1838.*

The Years of Growth

This was a period of remarkable change and development. At the beginning of the period, London already had a population of over one million; there were other large towns like Liverpool and Bristol; and the new industrial towns, like Bradford, which had had a population of only 13,000 in 1800, were just beginning to increase rapidly in size. But the majority of people still lived isolated lives, working as farm labourers or as artisans and craftsmen in small country towns. By the end of the period, however, many more people lived in the big towns and cities than in the country, working at a vast variety of new jobs created by the industrial revolution. More and more people were working in the mines to produce coal—the vital source of power for the new factories and locomotives, and the basis of the growing gas industry. New factories were being opened all the time, particularly in the north, making metal goods of every description. And as the towns swallowed up the surrounding countryside, more and more builders were needed to put up more houses. It became very common for boys to enter a trade different from that of their fathers. For girls, there were fewer changes in occupation. In 1871, nearly half of the working women were still employed as domestic servants—as they had been for years—and nearly one-third were working in textile factories or in the clothing trade.

Working conditions and wages for factory workers improved greatly during this period. This was partly because the workers now had their own organisations to represent their interests. In 1824, the Combination Act, which had prevented the formation of trade unions, was repealed. This led to the forming of a number of trade unions and culminated in the creation of Robert Owen's Grand National Consolidated Trades Union in 1833. But in the following year some Dorsetshire farm workers—the Tolpuddle Martyrs—were transported for administering 'illegal oaths' when they were forming an agricul-

'My Young Housemaid'.
Domestic work was one of the main occupations for women until modern times.

tural branch of the union. The whole project soon collapsed in a series of strikes and lock-outs.

A new and more successful attempt to form unions was made during the 1840s and the 1850s with the Miners' Association being founded in 1841 and the Amalgamated Society of Engineers in 1851. In 1868 the trades union congress, representing over 100,000 workers, met for the first time and three years later the unions were given greater legal recognition.

But at the beginning of the period conditions were still extremely bad by present-day standards. Many factory workers still laboured for 12 hours a day, or even more. In 1831, for example, workers in cotton factories started work at 5.30 a.m. or 6 a.m. and worked through until 7.30 p.m. or 8 p.m., with half an hour for breakfast, an hour for dinner, and half an hour for tea. But successive Factory Acts improved conditions and cut hours of work. In 1833, children under nine years of age were banned from working in textile factories and inspectors were appointed to see that this was carried out. As births were not registered until 1837, it was easy to evade this regulation, particularly as there were still only a handful of factory inspectors. In 1847 the hours of work for women in textile factories were reduced to 10 a day and in 1874–5 hours of work were again reduced, to 57 a week. There were a great number of different laws passed to regulate conditions in various industries, but in 1878 a Consolidating Act was passed, which attempted to bring some order into these separate pieces of legislation. By the end of the period some factory workers were working a nine-hour day.

Wages rose considerably. One estimate of the average annual wage for men in 1885 was £60 and there was a small minority of foremen and highly-skilled workmen and piece-rate workers who were earning £2 a week. But it is a little difficult to calculate true family incomes as they varied greatly with circumstances. A man was often comparatively well off when he was a bachelor living at home and earning a man's wage; he would be poor while his numerous children were growing up; better off again when his children started to work; and poor again when they had married and left home. Even by the middle of the century the family income of a typical town family, where all the children worked, could come to £3 or more a week.

A 14-year-old first offender in the Preston House of Correction told the chaplain there in 1851: 'Father is a weaver and gets 12s. weekly, besides 7s. 6d. for collecting for a burial club. He get drunk every Tuesday night after he comes from collecting. My eldest sister is a two-loom weaver and earns 17s. 6d. net. My next sister is a two-loom weaver, and gets 9s. 6d. Another sister is a dressmaker and gets 7s. or 8s. I got about 4s. or 5s. . . . I have a brother, a shoemaker, who gets about 12s.'

At that time, there were still many families in the cities living in utter want and destitution. In the same year, the Rev. J. Shearman, a domestic missionary in Bristol, described the children in one such family he had visited: 'The child is a pauper, sixpence a week and a loaf being its allowance. . . . The child runs about the street in rags, its head unacquainted with combing, its skin seldom washed, and its "young idea" about right and wrong very vague. . . . If a boy, he is sent forth with hearthstone, matches, or a "cadging" bag. . . . If a child is a female, and not wanted to stay with the younger ones, she ventures into the world with matches, or pins, or blacking, or firewood. . . .' Many of the poor drifted into crime, or were trained for it, while young, by their parents. In the middle of the nineteenth century, 1 in about every 150 of the population of England and Wales was estimated to be a criminal.

A new, menacing shadow hung over all the respectable poor who could not find a job or were too old to work. A Poor Law Amendment Act was passed in 1834 which

WHAT THEY ARE.

A London backyard slum in 1878.

ended the inefficient and corrupt Speen-hamland system. There was certain need for reform. The old system had encouraged improvidence among the poor and corruption amongst the overseers. But what re-replaced it was in a different way somewhat worse. Now the only official relief for the able-bodied poor was the workhouse.

In some of the old poorhouses, meals and living conditions had been better than they were outside; the new workhouses were more like prisons. In the middle of the century, the typical menu for the week might be bread and porridge for breakfast and supper, and suet pudding or bread and soup for dinner. Twice a week the inmates might have meat and potatoes for dinner. In former times, it had been accepted that 'the poor are always with us'; now, in the hard-working Victorian age, poverty had become almost an official crime. But once again there were many individuals who acted more charitably than the law allowed. Many of the Boards of Guardians set up to run the new system continued to provide outdoor relief to save the poor from the dreaded workhouse; they did so increasingly as the century went on. There were also a large number of town officials, churchgoers and other individuals who did much to relieve the distress amongst the poor by setting up soup kitchens for the unemployed and providing free breakfasts for schoolchildren in need.

Housing was another of the worst features of life in the Victorian age. In the centres of the towns huge, magnificent symbols of the wealth of the industrial age rose up in the shape of tall churches of many different sects, splendid, ornate railway stations, and huge neo-classical town halls—all brightly new and shining, but soon to be besmeared and begrimed by the sulphurous fumes belching out from the factory chimneys. In contrast, millions of people were herded into overcrowded insanitary tenements, or housed in small, cramped rows of depressingly similar back-to-back houses. But given the limited economic resources, and the enormous increase both in the general population and the

Coffee stall.
A familiar London street scene of the 1880s.

number living in cities, it is difficult to see how much more could have been done. Between 1801 and 1881 the population of England and Wales almost trebled in size—from about 9½ million to nearly 26 million.

As more and more people flocked into the new towns to find work the pressure upon accommodation became intense. In the parish of St. Pancras, in London, for example, there were 46,333 persons living in 5,826 houses in 1811. Twenty years later there were 103,548 residents and 12,369 houses. Because new houses could not be built fast enough, whole streets of what once had been respectable dwellings were transformed into slums.

There was a fairly general pattern to be observed in the decline of a street. The houses might have been built originally for society people in the eighteenth century. Then, a doctor or lawyer might set up his business in one of the houses. A public body might then take over one of the houses. It would be followed by a high-class shopkeeper, who would start trading from one of the houses. Other shopkeepers would move in. The rooms above the shop might be let to clerks or other white-collar workers. Other houses would then be divided off into rooms. And eventually, after perhaps a century or more, all middle-class owners would have moved out and the whole street of houses would have become tenements.

What were these mid-century slums like? The author of a survey of 'dwellings for the industrial classes' described one of the London tenements he visited in 1845 in the following terms: 'Near to St. George's Church, in the Borough, a narrow court was entered, numbering about a dozen houses. These houses are occupied by not less than from ten to twelve persons in each—they had no yards . . . they had no drains and the only privy that could be discovered was a square enclosed space in the centre of the court, undrained also. . . .' It was stated that landlords were making a profit of 15 to 30 per cent on their outlay. Each house was let at £20 a year. For a one-roomed, tiny hut with no ventilation at the back, and only a confined court in front, the rent was 2s. 9d. a week. But it was still home to some family.

The plight of the poor did not go completely unnoticed. During the second half of the century particularly—encouraged by Prince Albert—a number of determined attempts were made to provide better housing for the poor. One of the first philanthropists in the field was George Peabody, an American merchant living in London who put £150,000 in trust in 1862 for building five-storey-high blocks of flats for workers, with an inscription 'model houses for families' above the main entrance.

The really poor were not considered suitable tenants for these new respectable dwellings. As their tenements were torn down to make way for new blocks of flats, they had to move into already overcrowded tenements elsewhere. Up to 1830 or 1840 the poor had been fairly evenly distributed throughout London; but as the slums were pulled down

'Street Breakfast'.
A cartoon showing how the poor used to eat.

to make way for new houses and flats, the new railway lines and stations, churches, and office buildings, the poor started to drift out to the East End of London and the south. 'Once the poor dwellers in the heart of London could reach the West End by an easy walk," wrote Hugh MacCallum in 1883, 'but now we seldom see them there, for we have driven them too far away.' In addition to the social differences between classes, there was now a physical distance between them, too.

Nevertheless, by the end of the period there were many hundreds of thousands of 'respectable' working-class families living in reasonable comfort in small, but clean, terrace houses. The rooms were often tiny, and to make ends meet the family sometimes had a lodger living in the house, too. In spite of the cramped conditions, the manners of the time dictated that the front room, or parlour, should only be used on Sundays or on grand occasions such as funerals. The parlour would be better furnished than the other rooms. This was the age of ornaments and

Cheapside, 1846.
*In that year the wooden
pavement was taken up and
replaced by stone.*

Cheapside in the eighteenth century

knick-knacks. Even the poorest of these families would try to have a few cheap ornaments of Staffordshire pottery (now valuable collector's items) which flooded the market from the middle of the nineteenth century, or a plaster cast or group preserved from the earlier period.

Few houses had a bathroom. Every Saturday night, the tin bath was taken off its nail on the back wall of the house and placed in front of the kitchen range. Most of these houses were no longer lit by candles or by oil lamps—but by gas. At the beginning of the century, gas lighting had still been one of the marvels of the age. At public celebrations in Manchester, hundreds of people went to gaze in wonder at the crown on Philips and Lee's factory 'formed of gas lights, which from the pure flames emitted by that curious preparation, looked beautifully luminous'. Gas meters had been invented in 1815, though the wet meter, in which water was used to measure the volume of gas used, continued to give trouble for some time because the water froze in cold weather. And gas had been used experimentally for cooking in the 1830s. By the end of the period, it was in common use in the large cities. It was easier to light, too. The old tinder box had been replaced by matches, which were first made in Britain in 1826. To save money, however, many people had a spill vase or other receptacle on the mantelpiece containing twisted spills of paper which could be ignited at the kitchen fire.

There was also a great improvement in the variety and quality of food. An inquiry amongst the 'manufacturing people' in 1831 showed that 'potatoes, butter, sometimes pastry, sometimes bread, often oatcake, and occasionally, though rarely, a small sprinkling of bacon or other meat, constitute their dinner six days out of seven'. The basic food at that time was still bread, oatcake or bean and barley scones. By the middle of the century the development of railways and the greater availability of ice allowed fresh fish to be brought into the inland towns. Pickled herring, which had once been almost the only fish that any but the coastal dwellers ever knew, started to go out of fashion.

About 1870, tinned beef and mutton began to be imported from Australia and at the same time margarine started coming in from the United States and Holland. Though the margarine was rather tasteless and the tinned meat was often fat it was better than rancid butter and no meat—and only cost about half the price. Treacle had been popular for many years and about 1880 the first refined syrup started to appear. At the same time, cheap jam started to reach the shops. The jams often had very little connection with the names of the fruits on the labels, being made from vegetable pulp and flavourings. But their sweetness made them popular; bread and jam soon rivalled bread and treacle as one of the most popular meals. People were eating far more meat. Even by the middle of the century, the more prosperous workers expected to have a meal of meat and potatoes, or veal and ham pie once a day. And as time passed, bacon, eggs, and fish, including stewed eels, became increasingly obtainable and popular.

Clothing also improved. The production of cheap cotton goods in factories had increased so greatly that when Friedrich Engels visited Manchester in 1840 he found the working women there dressed almost entirely in cotton dresses. The men wore fustian trousers and jackets and cotton shirts. Most of these clothes were still made at home or bought second hand. The invention of the sewing machine changed all that. The first practical sewing machine of modern design was made by Isaac Merritt Singer in Boston, USA, in 1850. Seventeen years later, he opened his first overseas factory in Glasgow. Soon, factories in Britain were turning out thousand of cheap cotton clothes. At about the same time, boots and shoes started to be made in factories.

The wearing of cotton clothes increased personal cleanliness. Formerly the heavy woollen clothes had been difficult to wash and dry, so some people hardly ever bothered to do so. It was much easier to wash the light cotton clothes. The provision of better water supplies in the cities and the end of the soap tax in 1852 also helped. Clothes were washed by hand or boiled in a copper and pressed with a flat iron, heated on the kitchen range.

For some people the public house or gin palace remained the main source of pleasure. They opened very early in the morning and shut late at night. In 1831, according to one writer, it was customary for town workers to have a dram of gin on their way to work. Gin palaces opened at 7 a.m. or 8 a.m., even on Sundays; they would be full of customers drinking a 2d. glass of 'Old Tom'. Drunkenness had always been common. In the thirteenth century there had been drinking parties called scot-ales, condemned by many English bishops. But it was only with the growth of towns and the drinking of spirits that it became a grave social problem. Formerly, in the small isolated villages and country towns, drunkenness had been a local, almost a private, affair; now there were huge sections of the new industrial towns given over to drunken debauchery, particularly on Saturday nights and Sundays.

To fight this social evil, a number of temperance movements were started in the early part of the period. Many of these were run by middle-class people, but there were also a number of working-class reformers. Prominent among them was Joseph Livesey, a Baptist hand-loom weaver, who later became a cheese merchant. He was born in Preston, Lancs, in 1794, and in 1832, with six others, founded the Preston Temperance Society, whose members all signed a pledge never to take alcohol, except for medical reasons. They gave lectures, published magazines, and organised concerts as a counter-attraction to the pubs. From the beginning, temperance workers had concentrated a large part of their efforts on trying to reform drunkards, but an equally important part of their work was persuading children and young people not to fall into drunken habits. In 1847 a Band of Hope was formed in Leeds to provide temperance meetings for children and to encourage them to sign the pledge;

the movement soon spread to every part of the country.

Not all of the reformers, however, wanted people to stop drinking altogether. Many doctors and a number of organisations, such as Edinburgh University Temperance Society, favoured moderation in drinking. Some indication of the excessive drinking of the times can be found in the recommended limits prescribed by some reformers. In a lecture given in Hertford in 1877, Dr. Tasker Evans advocated that spirits should never be drunk except on medical advice, but 'a moderate quantity' of other drink could be taken—no more than two pints of beer, a half-pint of sherry or port, or a pint of claret or hock a day.

In 1830, in an attempt to reduce the drinking of gin, any householder in England was allowed to take out an excise licence for the sale of beer on or off the premises, without getting a licence from the local magistrates. This measure did not have the intended effect. The temperance movements and the Lord's Day Observance Society, which was founded in 1831, campaigned for greater legal restrictions on the sale of alcohol. In 1839 a clause in a Police Act stopped licensed houses in London from opening between midnight on Saturday and midday on Sunday. In 1861 a heavy tax was put on gin. And from 1869 all beer houses had to obtain a licence from the local magistrates again.

The biggest success came in the early 1870s when opening hours for public houses were made uniform in England. On Sundays, they were not allowed to open until 12.30 p.m. or 1 p.m. and they all had to shut in the afternoon. The hours on weekdays were, however, much more liberal. In London they could open from 5 a.m. to 12.30 p.m., in large towns from 6 a.m. to 11 p.m., and in other places from 6 a.m. to 10 p.m. In 1886 it was made illegal to sell liquor for consumption on the premises to children under the age of 13.

In spite of these changes, the effect on drunkenness was small. In fact, convictions for drunkenness actually rose between 1860 and 1875 and then started to decline from 76·87 per 10,000 of the population in 1875 to 59 per 10,000 in 1900.

Why was this? It is perhaps no coincidence that prices in general were often very high between 1860 and 1873. In 1873 they started to fall, so that by 1887 they were almost 40 per cent lower. People drank too much because they were poor and without hope. It was not drink that made them poor. The early temperance reformers were tackling the symptoms, not the cause.

But, almost incidentally, the temperance workers were responsible for some other very important reforms. While their criticisms were concentrated on just one aspect of society, their positive remedies were very widely spread. The 28 workers who established the 'Rochdale Equitable Pioneer Co-operative Society' were all temperance enthusiasts; Thomas Cook, secretary of the South Midlands Temperance Association, organised his first Cook's tour from Leicester to Loughborough on July 5, 1841—to a temperance demonstration. And another teetotaller turned tourist agent—John Frame —made the Highlands of Scotland popular for holidays.

The whole temperance movement was intimately connected with religion. Though no one church had a monopoly—there was a Church of England Temperance Society— the movement was especially strong amongst the Nonconformists. It was these churches, too, which attracted the most fervent working-class support. Some sects, like the Primitive Methodists, were almost entirely working class, while others, such as the Plymouth Brethren, founded in the 1820s by John Nelson Darby in Dublin, had a high proportion of working-class members. It was in the Nonconformist chapels and churches —Methodist, Unitarian, Baptist, Congregationalist—that many future working-class leaders received education, help, experience of public speaking, and faith in better times to come.

Many of the urban working class and the vast majority of the poor still remained completely untouched by religion of any kind. A church census taken one Sunday in March, 1851, showed that only about 40 per cent of the total population of England and Wales had gone to church. There were many who had genuine reasons for not going, but even allowing for these, it was estimated that over 5 million people—almost 30 per cent—had deliberately not attended a Sunday service.

It was in the poor, densely populated parts of big cities that absenteeism was highest. Partly, the reason was simply lack of churches. There just were not enough places in church to go round. Indeed, Parliament was persuaded to grant £1m. in 1818 for building churches in cities. In spite of the enormous amount of church and chapel building that went on, the problem was never solved. In St. Pancras, London, for example, a new parish church and three chapels were built between 1822 and 1831, but there were still only 13,800 church seats for a population of 103,548. What made the situation worse was the buying-up of pews by middle-class families. This, however, had little effect on the poor. It was mainly the middle classes, and perhaps just a handful of the upper working class, who considered it beneath their dignity to sit in one of the free seats if they could not have a pew permanently reserved for them.

The main reason so many of the urban workers stayed away from church was most probably because they believed that the established church was not for them—but for the middle class. It was for this reason that around the middle of the nineteenth century, churches of all sects started to open missions in the poorer parts of the cities. If the people would not go to church, the church would go to them. The culmination came in 1878 with the formation of the Salvation Army by William Booth. With its bands, and uniforms and rousing songs, it touched the hearts of some of the working class in a way that few of the conventional churches had ever done.

But just at the time when all sects were

trying to attract the urban workers and the poor into the churches, other leisure-time opportunities were developing which were to reduce attendance at church even further. Increasing wealth, leisure and freedom of movement were to improve the pattern of life for vast sections of the town workers out of all recognition. The biggest changes were made by the growth of railways, which gave ordinary people a chance to travel which they had never had before. In 1848 there were 5,000 miles of railways; and by 1885 there were 16,700. Cheap fares and special excursions gave people an opportunity to escape from the grim, depressing towns for a day. Even by 1850, cheap country excursions for children were common enough. But it was in the 1850s and the 1860s that excursion trips by train became really popular, particularly for visits to the Great Exhibition of 1851 and the second Exhibition 11 years later. In 1870 the excursion fare from London to Margate, Hastings or Dover was 3s. 6d. return. In 1872 the Midland Company started to provide third-class accommodation on all trains at 1d. a mile and two years later it abolished the second class and started to provide comfortable third-class travel at cheap rates for everyone. The other railway companies did the same.

People now had increasing leisure time in which to take advantage of these opportunities. In 1871 the Bank Holiday Act established Boxing Day, Easter Monday, White Monday and the first Monday in August as official holidays. The week-end had become longer, too. The Factory Act of 1850 had prohibited textile factories from using their machinery after 2 p.m. on Saturdays. The 5½-day week gradually became general for both men and women in many industries, though not in shops or on the farms. From the 1880s, too, a few manual workers began to get a week's paid holiday every year.

More gentle amusements started to replace the savage pleasures of the past. Bull-baiting was made illegal in 1835 and cock-fighting in 1849, though they continued secretly in some places, particularly in the North, until the 1880s. By the middle of the century, reformers were already suggesting what should take the place of these cruel sports. In 1847 one writer said that three bodily recreations which might be uniformly provided for the poor were 'various kinds of innocent games, amongst which cricket would of course hold a foremost place; the amusement of a garden; and the luxury of bathing'.

Attendance at cricket matches then was not entirely disinterested as it was still very much associated with betting. Matches began to attract a new kind of spectator after the county championships started in 1873. The first Test match against the Australians was played in Melbourne in 1877. Football matches were equally popular. The Football Association was formed in 1863 and soon a visit to a football match became one of the most popular Saturday afternoon entertainments for men. Gardens were still only a dream for many town dwellers; it was not until the development of council housing that they became at all common. But the development of the railways made it possible for far more people to go to the seaside for a day's trip or even for a week's holiday, at such resorts as Blackpool, Margate or Brighton.

Changes in the country during this period were much slower than they were in the towns. From the middle of the century there was probably a steady flow of people from the country to the towns. The draining off of the more ambitious left the country even more neglected. Wages, even including allowances of all kinds, were lower in the country than in the towns.

Although we hear a great deal about bad housing in the towns, it was just as bad in many ways in the country. A hundred years ago, some cottages still had earthen floors, only one room in which the whole family slept, and open rafters covered with a piece of cloth to keep out the rain. Oil lamps had replaced candles for artificial lighting. At first, whale oil was used, but in the 1860s paraffin became more common.

Bathing Place at Ramsgate.
*An eighteenth century artist's
view.*

Sea bathing at Bridlington Bay.
*By 1813 bathing had become
more decorous.*

New cottages were built in some places in the 1860s and 1870s. This followed the Prince of Wales's purchase and development of the royal estate at Sandringham, where he put up a number of model cottages for farm workers. Many of the big landowners copied his example. Country clothing was old-fashioned. Well after the middle of the 19th century many of the men still wore rough smock-frocks, white hats and leather leggings. Hours of work were longer, holidays shorter, opportunities for education and entertainment fewer than they were in the towns. It was only when elementary education became compulsory for all that opportunities for country and town children began to become more equal.

Although a Test match was not played in 1887, two artists painted a picture showing the two teams of real-life players they would have chosen for the match.

Albury Street.
A poor area of London in 1911.

Modern Times

Even in the most recent times, poverty has not been entirely abolished in Britain. But there has been a great change both in the nature of the poverty itself and in the attitudes towards it. The number of poor people is now much smaller than it once was and they are relatively rich compared with the poor people of the 1880s. Furthermore, from the beginning of the modern period there have been many people—sociologists, clergymen, union leaders, journalists, politicians—who have exposed the misfortunes and the miseries of the poor. People no longer consider the poor to be disgraceful but consider it disgraceful that poverty should exist in such a rich country.

At the beginning of the period, in the large cities, there were still millions living in desperate poverty. Charles Booth, after careful inquiry in London, estimated that families, earning less than 18s. a week—11 per cent of the total—were living in 'chronic want'. Another 23 per cent, earning between 18s. and 21s., were living in poverty. In 1883 one writer estimated that there were 2 million poor people in London out of a population of 4 million. And in 1885 another writer claimed that out of half a million Board School children in London not more than 10 per cent were sufficiently fed. These

were unscientific estimates, but there is no doubt that poverty was widespread both in London and in the other major cities.

On the whole, it was unskilled workers in factories, those working in declining industries, such as nail-making, and those in 'sweated' industries, who were poor. Some of the lowest wages were paid to people who worked at home. In the 1880s W. C. Preston found that workers were paid 2¼d. a gross for match-box making. They could make 500 to 600 in a day. Tailoring was another of the 'sweated' industries. For trouser-finishing— sewing in linings, making button-holes and stitching on buttons— the payment was 2½d. a pair. The rate for finishing men's shirts was 10d. a dozen.

Wages were just as low and conditions just as bad in many of the smaller factories in the North. In the late 1890s R. H. Sherard wrote

Cheapside, 1900.
A photograph taken just before the start of the motor-car age.

a series of articles on 'The White Slaves of England' which created quite a stir both at home and abroad. He described the 'slave-like' conditions under which nailmakers, white lead workers, slipper makers, woolcombers and chainmakers still worked. According to him there were still women forging chain harrows for 14 hours a day at Cradley Heath, Staffs., for 6s. a week.

The narrow borderline between poverty and relative comfort was always changing, as trades declined or unemployment grew. In London, W. C. Preston found a French-polisher who had been unable to get a week's work all that winter. 'He has a wife and five children; all are decent, respectable people. They have to live on bread and a halfpenny-worth of treacle for days together and to content themselves with one or two pennyworth of coal or coke at a time.' Many of the unemployed came to London to seek work. Those who did not find it had to sleep out— not so much on the iron benches of the Embankment, where it was far too cold—but more on the recessed seats of London Bridge, huddled together for warmth, or underneath the railway arches. They were too poor—or too proud—to spend the night in a 2d. bed in a 'dosshouse', containing 60 or more beds in each dormitory.

But even by the beginning of the modern period there had been a remarkable change for the better. The majority of people were not living in these conditions. Booth found that 42 per cent had a regular wage of between 22s. and 30s. a week, which was high enough to protect them from actual poverty. And there were another 13 per cent, earning 30s. to 50s. a week, who were relatively well off. These included foremen and skilled workers, such as compositors in the printing trade, and the more skilled workers in engineering. They would have enough money to save in the Post Office Savings Bank—which was founded in 1861—and they might even be buying their home, particularly in the provinces. Entry into these favoured jobs was guarded jealously; it was often restricted to sons who had fathers in the trade.

One of the biggest changes was in the occupations, and the status, of women. At the beginning of the period most women still worked as domestic servants or in the textile or clothing trades; middle-class girls might work as nurses, governesses, or teachers. Office and shop workers were still predominantly men. It was the invention of the typewriter which played a big part in the emancipation of women.

Although a machine had been patented by an English engineer, Henry Mill, in 1714, it was not until 1873 that the first commercial typewriter was marketed by the American firm of Remington. The YMCA in New York organised the first courses to train 'lady typewriters', as typists were then called. The typewriter was being sold in England in 1874. A Remington office was opened in London in 1886 and special training schools were set up. In 1888 two typists started work in the Inland Revenue Department in London and within a few years girls started to be employed as typists by more and more business firms.

At the same time women started demanding equality in the political sphere. A Bill to give votes to women was introduced into the House of Commons in 1886, but it was defeated. Agitation continued until the First World War, with militants such as Emmeline Pankhurst and others using violent means—such as breaking shop windows—to achieve their ends. During the First World War, women took over many of the men's jobs. Public sympathy swung towards them and in 1918 women over 30 were given the vote, and 10 years later they were all given the same voting rights as men.

Even before the First World War the first small steps had been taken towards the present system of social security. In 1908, old age pensions of 5s. a week were granted to people over 70 whose annual income was less than £21. In 1909 Labour Exchanges were set up. And in 1911 a National Insur-

Women Clerks.
An early photograph showing office girls at work in the Post Office.

ance Act was introduced which gave 7s. a week unemployment benefit to workers in seven industries.

The system broke down under the successive strains of the slump of the early 1920s and the world-wide depression which started in 1929 and caused unemployment to reach a peak of 3¾ million in September, 1932. In 1935 a means test was introduced under which the whole of the family's earnings were taken into account before relief for unemployment was given. The rates were low —24s. a week for a married couple and 3s. to 6s. a week for each child.

Another great social change in modern times has been in the altered attitude towards the home. 'Home, sweet home' had been the focal point of the lives of the newly rich middle-class families in the Victorian era. The pleasures and the virtues of the home were extolled by many lecturers and writers, such as C. Northcote who conducted mother's meetings in the villages of southern England. In *Talks with Mothers*, published in 1894, it was stated: 'One of the prettiest sights in the world is to see the father coming home from his work and the mother with the baby in her arms, and perhaps other children clustering round, standing at the door or garden gate to welcome him home, and he takes the baby who crows with delight to see 'Daddy' home again. . . . This is a pleasant picture. . . . But, alas! there is another far too common one. The father coming home, but the children cowering away in the corners to be if possible, out of his sight, and the poor wife only too glad if she too can escape his notice.'

Poor housing was one of the main causes of these family troubles. The worst parts of the cities were often known as the Rookeries. W. C. Preston describes one he visited in the 1880s where the courts were filled with an accumulation of sewage and refuse, and there was no cleansing water—but only rotten staircases and dark, filthy passages swarming with vermin. The average size of many rooms was 8 feet square. The walls and ceilings were black with filth. The beds were sometimes made of rough boards resting on bricks, but often of rubbish and rags. A sanitary inspector had found living together in one cellar in London a father, a mother, three children—and four pigs. Many of the residents of the Rookeries were street hawkers. They kept the rotting fish or stale vegetables they had failed to sell in their rooms overnight. Others worked as furriers pulling skins from rabbits, dogs, rats and other animals.

There was considerable public concern about these conditions. A Royal Commission on the Housing of the Working Classes which reported in 1885 had the Prince of Wales (later King Edward VII) as one of its members. The Commission heard about many places all over the country which were just as bad, or even worse, than those that Preston had described. But very little was done to alter these conditions. Housing Acts were passed which authorised local councils to clear slums and gave them powers of compulsory purchase; but the Government refused to subsidise housing. Before the First World War, very few council houses were built. It was private enterprise which showed what could be done.

As early as 1853, Sir Titus Salt, a Bradford millowner, had started to build the 'model village' of Saltaire, near Shipley, for his employees, but even greater attention was attracted by some later developments. 'Model villages' were founded by W. H. Lever (later Lord Leverhulme) at Port Sunlight, Birkenhead, in 1888, by George Cadbury at Bournville, Birmingham, and by Joseph Rowntree at New Earswick, York, in 1904. In 1903, however, there was a completely new kind of development, which was both more revolutionary in approach and far more ambitious in its scope. In that year, Sir Ebenezer Howard helped to found the first garden city at Letchworth, Herts. It differed from the preceding 'model villages' in that it was a completely self-contained town cut off from surrounding towns by a protective belt of farmland or open country. In 1920 a second garden city was founded at Welwyn: these were the predecessors of the post-war new towns.

These ventures provided houses such as workers had never lived in before, with bathrooms and an adequate number of rooms. At Letchworth every house had its own garden and no worker lived more than a mile from the factory where he worked. Over 1,000 cottages were built at Letchworth before the First World War and more houses were added when the war was over.

But these benefits were available to only a very few people. It was not until 1919 that local councils were given Government subsidies to build houses. Even then, building costs were so high and the demand for houses so great that very few workers, except the most skilled artisans, could afford to pay the rents charged.

In 1924 another Housing Act was passed which allowed councils to build more homes. Building costs and interest rates had both fallen, so that rents were much lower and within the reach of a much larger number of manual workers. But the very poor were still excluded. It was not until 1930 that a major start was made on clearing slums. To ease overcrowding in the centres of the cities, councils started to build blocks of flats from the mid-thirties, but usually only five or six storeys high.

The pulling down of slums and the rehousing of the inhabitants was not universally welcomed. Many critics claimed that it was a pointless task as the tenants of the new homes would never wash but would use their baths for storing coal. But, as the Ministry of Health observed in a 1938 report, 'we know now that as a general proposition these dismal prophecies were wrong'. The vast majority of people lived a better life as new homes gave them the chance to do so.

The concentration of slum clearance in the towns made many people forget that there were just as many slums in the country —particularly in the more remote areas. In 1939 it was found that there were still country cottages in Wales with small windows

Bournville model houses. *Working class accommodation of a higher standard than ever before, but the bath was still in the kitchen.*

that did not open, damp walls, floors made of mud and no sanitation.

Many houses were destroyed by bombing during the Second World War, when all house-building stopped. To overcome the scarcity of houses after the end of the war, prefabricated houses were put up, designed originally to last for 10 years. But house-building did not keep pace with demand and some 'prefabs' are still inhabited. Earlier marriages, the increased population, and the universal desire to live in one's own home and not with parents, have made the demand for housing even greater. Many slums have been pulled down, but there are still about 3 million old homes which need to be replaced.

Other developments during this period made it much more pleasant for people to stay at home. Between the wars, the amount of mass-produced furniture started to increase: it was the age of the three-piece suite. Though much of the furniture by present-day standards was poor in design and quality, it was cheap; the average-sized home could be furnished for £50. Hire purchase made it easier for ordinary people to buy new furniture, though many people still feared to do so, as before the war their furniture could be taken away if they fell into arrears with their weekly payments. Many people therefore, even in their new homes, had to make do with improvised furniture, such as wooden orange crates instead of kitchen cupboards, and bare floorboards in every room.

Between the wars, food was plentiful, cheap, and more wholesome than it had ever been before. The very poorest had a diet consisting mainly of bread, strong tea, fish and chips, soup, and sometimes meat. But most people had a much greater variety. There was usually a joint of meat on Sundays, which could be bought at a reduced price on Saturday night when the stall-holders in the markets sold off their meat cheaply. The meat was eaten cold on Monday, which was usually also washing day. On other days of the week, there were sausages, pies, fish and chips, or an economical dish such as stew or Lancashire hotpot. To add savour to the rather tasteless English cooking, there was always a bottle of sauce, rich with spices, on the table. Many of the present-day sauce manufacturers were well established by the beginning of the modern period. Fruit was cheap and there were more exotic, tasty tinned fruits, such as mandarin oranges, which could be bought in the markets for 2d. a tin. There were biscuits of all kinds and loose broken biscuits were sold at half the price of regular brands. Food was bought at markets and small shops; there were no supermarkets until the 1950s.

In the home itself there was much more for people to do. Now that almost everyone could read, modern newspapers and magazines started to appear. They were written specially for the new mass audience. The magazine *Titbits*—a collection of extracts from books, newspapers and other magazines —was brought out by George Newnes in 1881. It soon had a sale of 1 million copies. In 1896 the *Daily Mail* appeared. It was the first popular style newspaper, even though it still had advertisements on the front page, like the old-style newspapers. It cost only ½d. The *Daily Express* was started four years later and in 1903 came the *Daily Mirror*, not

The Coffee House.
Newspapers were so expensive in the eighteenth century that even the well-to-do used to go to coffee houses to read them.

the paper as it is today, but a newspaper for gentlewomen.

It was this generation that discovered the pleasures of reading—not only newspapers and magazines, but also books, which were now far more widely available. Although the first Public Libraries Act had been passed in 1850, it was not until 1919 that the limit of a 1d. rate for the library service was abolished. County Councils were free to set up public libraries in all areas that did not have one. The paperback revolution also began. There were already such series as 'Benn's Sixpenny Library', but the real change came in 1935 when Allen Lane (later Sir Allen) started Penguin Books. Initially it produced reprints of worthwhile fiction in paperback form at 6d. a volume. More than 100 titles

TIT-BITS

FROM ALL THE MOST INTERESTING
BOOKS. PERIODICALS AND NEWSPAPERS IN THE WORLD

No. I.—Vol. I. [ENTERED AT STATIONERS' HALL.] PRICE ONE PENNY. [REGISTERED FOR TRANSMISSION ABROAD.] OCT. 22, 1881.

"TIT-BITS."

THERE is no paper in the world conducted on the lines which will be followed in *Tit-Bits*. It will be a production of all that is most interesting in the books, periodicals, and newspapers of this and other countries. Opinions may differ as to whether it is fair for newspapers to use other people's writings so extensively as has now become the practice. Whatever fault may be found by some with this whole-sale abstracting, in the case of *Tit-Bits* it is at any rate done openly and avowedly, and no attempt is made to pass off extracts as original compositions. There is scarcely a newspaper which does not give some extracts. The business of the conductors of *Tit-Bits* will be like that of the dentist—an organised system of extracting; but instead of, like the dentist, extracting that which is bad, and leaving that which is good, they will pursue exactly the opposite course, and extract that which is good, and leave the remainder. A complete system has been arranged whereby all the most interesting papers and books of England, France, Germany, Italy, Russia, America, Australia, and the Indies will be regularly searched, and whatever is found of interest to the general reader—in short, wherever a tit-bit is discovered—it will be drafted into the new paper *Tit-Bits*. It is impossible to find a person who can read the English language who will not be entertained by reading *Tit-Bits*. *Tit-Bits* will contain interesting incidents, amusing anecdotes, pithy paragraphs. Any person who takes in *Tit-Bits* for three months will at the end of that time be an entertaining companion, as he will then have at his command a stock of smart sayings and a fund of anecdote which will make his society agreeable. It is impossible for any man in the busy times of the present to even glance at any large number of the immense variety of books and papers which have gone on accumulating, until now their number is fabulous. It will be the business of the conductors of *Tit-Bits* to find out from this immense field of literature the best things that have ever been said or written, and weekly to place them before the public for one penny.

AN officer, not remarkable for courage, came one day to Quin, the actor, and asked him what he should do after having had his nose pulled. "Why, sir," said Quin, "soap your nose for the future, and then they'll slip their hold."

WHEN last the Queen was about to be confined the Prince Consort said to one of his little boys: "I think it is very likely, my dear, that the Queen will soon present you with a little brother or sister—which do you prefer?" The child (pausing): "Well, I think, if it is the same to mamma, I should prefer a pony."

A WILD young fellow, who was staying at a country house, was asked by a refined young lady to write some poetry in her album about autumn. The following was his performance:—

"The melancholy days have come,
The saddest of the yeer;
It's a little too warm for whisky hot,
And a little too cold for beer."

MR. FALLS, a well-known sportsman, happened one day to ride down a hound. The irascible but witty master of the Quorn attacked him in no measured language. "Sir," was the reply, "I'd have you recollect that I am Mr. Falls, of Dungannon." The answer was ready: "I don't care if you are the Falls of Niagara, you shan't ride over my hounds."

THE Chancellor of the Duchy of Lancaster was dining with a well-known citizen of Cottonopolis, and the conversation turned on the subject of the growth and development of America. "I should like," said the host, who is an enthusiastic admirer of the great Republic, "to come back fifty years after my death to see what a fine country America had become." "I believe you will be glad of any excuse to come back," said Mr. Bright.

AN Englishman in Paris went into a restaurant to get his dinner. Unacquainted with the French language, yet unwilling to show his ignorance, he pointed to the first line on the bill of fare, and the polite waiter brought him a plate of thin soup. This was very well, and when it was despatched he pointed to the second line. The waiter understood him perfectly, and brought him a vegetable soup. "Rather more soup than I want," thought he; "but it is a Paris fashion." He duly pointed to the third line, and a plate of tapioca broth was brought him. Again, to the fourth line, and was furnished with a bowl of preparation of arrow-root. He tried the fifth line, and was supplied with some gruel kept for invalids. The bystanders now supposed that they saw an unfortunate individual who had lost all his teeth, and our friend, determined to get as far from the soup as possible, pointed in despair to the last line on the bill of fare. The intelligent waiter, who saw at once what he wanted, politely handed him a bunch of toothpicks. This was too much, the Englishman paid his bill and left.

IT is computed that the average circumference of a woman's waist is 36in. It is also computed that the average length of a man's arm is 36in. Great is thy wisdom, oh Nature!

A VERY loquacious female witness, whom the opposing counsel could not silence, so far kept at bay, that by way of browbeating her he exclaimed, "Why, woman, there's brass enough in your face to make a kettle." "And sauce enough in yours," she instantly rejoined, "to fill it."

SAID Lord John Russell to Hume, at a social dinner: "What do you consider the object of legislation?" "The greatest good to the greatest number." "What do you consider the greatest number?" continued his lordship. "Number one, my lord," was the commoner's prompt reply.

"Now, then, my hearties," cried a gallant Yankee captain, seeing that it was all over with his men, "fight like heroes till your powder's done; then run for your lives. I'm a little lame, I'll start now."

IT is doubtful whether human eccentricity ever went further than in the case of Lord Holland, who was contemporaneous with William the Third. It was his usual custom to regale his stud of horses with a weekly concert. He had a gallery erected for the purpose, and he maintained that the music cheered their hearts and improved their tempers.

THE son-in-law of a Chancery barrister having succeeded to the lucrative practice of the latter, came one morning in breathless ecstasy to inform him that he had succeeded in bringing nearly to its termination a cause which had been pending in that court of scruples for several years. Instead of obtaining the expected congratulations of the retired veteran of the law, his intelligence was received with indignation. "It was by this suit," exclaimed he, "that my father was enabled to provide for me and to portion your wife, and with the exercise of common prudence it would have furnished you with the means of providing handsomely for your children and grandchildren."

A STORY is told of a graceless scamp who gained access to the Clarendon printing office, in Oxford, when the formes of a new edition of the Episcopal Prayer Book had just been made up, and were ready for the press. In that part of the "forme" containing the marriage service, he substituted the letter "k" for the letter "v" in the word live, and thus the vow to "love, honour, etc., as long as ye both shall live," was made to read, "so long as ye both shall like." The change was not discovered until the whole of the edition was printed off. If the sheets thus rendered useless in England be still preserved, it would be a good speculation to have them neatly bound and forwarded to Indiana and Connecticut.

First issue of Tit-Bits.
The magazine that brought reading to the masses.

Eastbourne Lending Library.
*Public libraries provided
reading for all, but in pre-war
days many of them still had a
'closed' system, with none of the
books on display.*

were published in the first two years. Then in 1937 Pelican Books was started to provide serious non-fiction literature at the same price. Almost anyone, including those who had had to leave school at 14, could now afford to build up their own library. More formal education was provided by the Workers' Educational Association, founded by Albert Mansbridge in 1903, and by university extension courses. At the beginning of the Second World War there were nearly 60,000 adult students taking these high-level courses. And at Oxford, there was Ruskin College, the working man's own college, founded by two Americans in 1899.

For home entertainment, many people already possessed a gramophone which had to be laboriously wound up by hand. Much greater entertainment, and instruction, was provided by the radio. The British Broad-

casting Company (as it then was) began transmissions in November, 1922. Radio became popular immediately. By 1926 there were already 2 million licence holders, and hundreds of thousands more who listened, but did not pay. The first receivers were crystal sets. These cost only 7s. 6d. while the headphones cost another 2s. or so. They were soon replaced by battery sets with an accumulator which had to be taken to the electrician's shop every week or fortnight to be recharged.

Television also started before the last war. The first transmissions were made from Alexandra Palace in August, 1936, but only 20,000 sets were sold before the outbreak of the last war, when all transmissions stopped. The growth of a mass TV audience is a product of the post-war years.

Before the last war some people made their

own radio, or wireless, sets. It was cheaper to do so—and more fun. This period saw the real beginning of the age of hobbies: gardening, fretwork, model-making, stamp collecting and many more. As wages rose and people had more leisure they could afford to pursue their individual interests.

One of the most popular activities was keeping a pet of some kind. Public exhibitions of sports involving cruelty to animals had become a thing of the past. The Royal Society for the Prevention of Cruelty to Animals helped to stamp out cases of private maltreatment of animals. Ordinary people could afford to indulge the particular British interest in pets and animals, so that today practically every home has a pet of some kind. There are about 4 million dogs, over 6 million cats and 8 or 9 million pet birds in Britain.

In clothing, there were also drastic changes. Before the First World War, many men still wore suits of cotton corduroy or mole-skin, second-hand clothes, or 'reach-me-downs'—so called because the shop assistant had to reach down these ready-made clothes from the shelves where they were stacked. They 'fitted where they touched'. A man's occupation or native country was often revealed by his clothes. Many miners wore bell-bottomed trousers, while bricklayers wore heavy colourful clothes, rather like the costermongers. Lancastrian men liked brightly-coloured clothes, while the youth of Tyneside were renowned as 'sharp dressers'.

All this was to be changed when multiple tailors started. In 1900 Montague Burton opened his business in Leeds and within 10 years he had a chain of stores in the North where cheap, stylish, made-to-measure suits could be bought. His business—and others—expanded rapidly after the end of the First World War. In the 1920s Burton House was opened in New Oxford Street, London. Men became better dressed than they had ever been before, in lounge suits with neatly creased trouser legs, which had been popularised by King Edward VII when he was

Crystal sets.
Before the last war, the new invention of radio brought pleasure to many millions.

Prince of Wales. The blue serge suit was very common. In the late thirties, some of the younger men started going without a cap or hat and changed their hair style from a centre to a side parting. And they started wearing belts instead of braces to keep their trousers up and discarded sock suspenders.

There were even greater changes in the appearance of women. After the First World War, for the first time ever, women's skirts became short, until in the mid-twenties they had reached the knees. Rayon, or artificial silk stockings, became popular at the same time. It was at that time too that cosmetics, such as lipstick and rouge, came into general use. Before the First World War, it had been considered improper to use cosmetics, except for face powders which were produced in different shades. The first 'permanent wave' was given by Charles Nessler, a German living in London, in 1906; previously, the Marcel wave which gave a natural wavy effect to hair had been invented by a French hairdresser. But it was not until the inter-war years that 'perms' became at all common,

Canterbury Hall, Lambeth.
A music hall of the 1850s.

and even then they were too expensive for many women and girls, except for very special occasions. Instead, they curled their hair with rags, curlers, or curling tongs heated in the fire. The Eton crop was succeeded by a longer, naturally wavy hair style, which in its turn was replaced at the beginning of the last war by the pageboy look in which the hair was curled underneath at the back. Many women and girls made their own clothes at home; quite a number of homes now had their own sewing machine, usually bought on hire purchase. But chain stores, like Marks and Spencers, were already making cheap, good-quality clothes more widely available.

Outside the home, too, there were many more opportunities for amusement and entertainment. Drunkenness continued to decline, with convictions falling from 59 per 10,000 of the population in England and Wales at the beginning of the twentieth century to 20·18 in 1925. Pubs remained popular. But from the 1900s they became increasingly, not mere drinking dens, but respectable places where a man could take his wife. There were many other places now for drinking, particularly working men's clubs and the music halls.

The music halls had started in the saloon theatres attached to many public houses in the middle years of the nineteenth century.

But, as their popularity increased, they became separate establishments. Just before the First World War there were 48 music halls in London alone and each of the major provincial towns had a number, too. Many of the stars, such as Little Tich, Vesta Tilley, George Robey, Harry Lauder, Marie Lloyd and Harry Champion—to mention only a few—became household names. The programme consisted of sketches, juggling acts, dancing, comic turns and songs—sentimental, such as 'A Bicycle Made for Two' sung by Miss Katie Lawrence, and patriotic, such as 'Sons of the Sea' sung by Mr. Arthur Reece and 'The Old Tattered Flag' sung by Miss Bessie Bonehill. Some of the stars were to retain their popularity after the end of the First World War, and a few after the end of the Second World War, but the music hall was soon to die. It was killed by the cinema.

The first public motion picture performance was given in London in the 1890s. Even before the First World War a number of spectacular films such as *Queen Elizabeth*, 1912, and *Quo Vadis*, 1913, had already been made. The main emphasis, however, particularly in Hollywood, was on comedy, with such performers as Mack Sennett, Fatty Arbuckle and Charlie Chaplin, who made his first film for Keystone in 1914. But the cinema industry really developed after the First World War, particularly after 'talkies' began in the late 1920s. All over the country, huge cinemas were opened, furnished and equipped with a munificence that ordinary people had rarely experienced before, and where the spectator could see two films, and sometimes a stage show, all for 3d. or in the best seats for 6d. or 1s. at the most. A visit to the cinema became the highlight of many people's week. Stars such as Greta Garbo were to be admired by many men and imitated by thousands of girls. Everyone had heard of Marlene Dietrich, Clark Gable, Norma Shearer, Ginger Rogers, Douglas Fairbanks, Jean Harlow—and Mickey Mouse. As an alternative to the cinema, there were in the bigger towns the local 'palais de danse', where couples in their thousands flocked every Saturday night.

There has also been a great improvement in the standard of public catering. At the beginning of the period there were in London only expensive restaurants, dingy coffee houses, or 'slap bangs' which served beer, coffee, tea and doubtful food. In 1894 Lyons opened their first teashop in Piccadilly. Within two years 17 had been opened, and by 1939 there were about 200 in London and another 50 in provincial cities. The first Corner House was opened in Coventry Street in 1909.

One of the distinctive features of these restaurants was the emphasis on hygiene and cleanliness, which extended also to the waitresses. The 'nippies', as they were called, wore a uniform consisting of a black dress with white collar, cuffs and apron. They also wore a black and white cap. Though the first tea-shops were patronised mainly by middle-class mothers and daughters from

Pre-war 'Nippies'.
They worked at J. Lyons's tea shops which provided good food and efficient service at popular prices.

Bathing Pond, Tooting Common.
The opening ceremony in 1906.

the suburbs, the tea-shops soon attracted customers from other classes, too.

At the week-ends many thousands of people left the overcrowded cities for the quietness of the countryside or the excitements of the seaside. Many people, particularly young workers from the factories, offices and shops, went out on their bicycles. The 'bike' gave people a freedom of individual movement such as they had never experienced before. There had been 'boneshakers' in the 1860s, which were succeeded in the next decade by the penny-farthing, with its large wheel in front and small wheel behind. In the 1880s the safety cycle as we know it today had been invented and so had the pneumatic tyre by John Boyd Dunlop, a Scottish veterinary surgeon, who took out a patent for his invention in 1888.

By the turn of the century, according to a book of advice called *Enquire Within*, cycling had become 'a great favourite with the ladies. . . . Given a modest and well-made costume, a lady's figure is shown to great advantage if she is a graceful rider.' But cycling then was not without its mishaps. 'A broken crank is a very awkward dilemma, and is generally due to a flaw in the metal. The only thing to be done is to tie the crank up with string, and make for the nearest railway station. . . .' Apart from such misfortunes, people could at last go miles away from home in comfort—and all for nothing but the initial price of the machine. Thousands took to the roads every week-end.

There were cars, too. F. W. Lanchester built the first British car with a petrol-driven engine in 1896, though there had been foreign cars before that. In 1896, too, the speed limit for cars and 'horseless carriages' was raised from 4 .m.p.h. to 12 m.p.h. and it was no longer necessary to have a man with a red flag walking in front of them. By 1914 there were 123,000 motor-cars, lorries and

Paris-Motor-Car Excursions - TH. COOK & FILS
Excursions en Automobile à Paris   1, Place de l'Opéra, Paris

Héliotypie E. Le Deley, Paris

Seeing Paris.
An early Cook's motor-car
excursion around 'gay Paree'.

taxis in Britain and by 1939 there were over 2 million private cars. Most of them were owned by the middle classes, though the skilled worker might be able to afford to run a small second-hand car. But coach trips and excursions were now very popular with the working classes. Transport in and around the towns was better too, with buses, trams and, in London, from 1890 onwards the first real Tube train, running under the river Thames from King William Street to Stockwell.

By 1939 it was estimated that one in three of all working-class people earning £4 a week or less were going away for an annual holiday. The cheapest form of holiday was provided by the Youth Hostels Association, founded in 1929, which provided beds in their hostels for 1s. a night and cooking facilities for those who could not afford to pay for a meal. But most families went to stay with relatives, or at a cheap boarding house at the seaside—with its pier and pierrot shows. Just before the last war a new form of luxury holiday had started which was to become increasingly popular. In 1937 the first Butlin's holiday camp was opened at Skegness. By 1939 it was estimated that there were 200 holiday camps in all—including the very small ones—but because prices were still relatively high they tended to be patronised more by the office workers than the factory workers. The growth of holidays abroad, trips in the car, and mass entertainment is mainly a development of the last 10 years.

Though there are still layers of relative poverty—particularly amongst old people—in Britain today, there have been spectacular changes in living conditions, general wealth, opportunities and freedom of movement in the last two centuries. These have been brought about mainly by the industrial revolution, which has resulted in a shift from a predominantly country-based population,

65

just about able to feed itself except in times of stress caused by bad harvests or by war, to a much more affluent, city-dwelling population. These vast changes were not unassociated in the early stages with considerable hardships, but the long-term result has been materially beneficial to practically all classes. The wealth provided by the technical, scientific and managerial revolutions in industry has by no means solved all problems, indeed it has created some of its own. But, for the first time ever, the majority of people can now live in clean, comfortable homes, well equipped and furnished, with opportunities for travel, entertainment and the pursuit of hobbies and interests such as they have never had before. Not all people live in this way. But it is no longer accepted that the problems of the submerged poor—even though they are a much smaller segment of the population than they ever were before—are of no interest or concern to society as a whole.

'Cook's Tour'.
An early tour to the Holy Land,
about 1880.

4. CRIME AND WARS

The Georgian Age

During this period the individual was often treated with extreme brutality; but there was little mass cruelty. The only mass destruction occurred when thousands died during the periodic plagues. These plagues were not caused by man—only by his ignorance. So, in searching for a cause, man attributed the plagues to God. They were a punishment for men's sins. The age was full of prophecies of doom. In April, 1750, a soldier predicted that London was about to be destroyed, and the Bishop of London called on all sinners to repent in a best-selling pamphlet of which 100,000 copies were soon sold.

People who offended against the laws were dealt with harshly. The normal punishment for a felony was death. Executions were held in public before shouting, fighting, screaming mobs, who looked upon the event as a holiday. Writing in the 1740s, Samuel Richardson described the execution of five men at Tyburn in London. 'That I might better view the Prisoners, and escape the Pressure of the Mob, which is prodigious, nay, almost incredible, if we consider the Frequency of these Executions in London, which is once a month, I mounted my Horse, and accompanied the melancholy Cavalcade from Newgate to the fatal Tree.' The route from Newgate Prison was so crowded with spectators that the cart taking the prisoners to the gallows had to be stopped every 20 or 30 yards to clear a way. He went on: 'At the place of execution a psalm was sung amidst the curses and quarrelling of hundreds of the most abandon'd and profligate of mankind. . . .

'As soon as the poor Creatures were half-dead, I was much surprised, before such a Number of Peace-Officers, to see the Populace fall to hauling and pulling the Carcases with so much earnestness, as to occasion several warm Rencounters and broken Heads. These, I was told, were the Friends of the Person executed, or such as, for the sake of the Tumult, chose to appear so, and some Persons sent by Private Surgeons to obtain Bodies for Dissection. . . .

'One of their Bodies was carried to the Lodging of his Wife, who not being in the way to receive it, they immediately hawked it about to every Surgeon they could think of; and when none would buy it, they rubbed Tar all over it, and left it in a Field hardly cover'd with Earth.'

The executions were held at Tyburn every month. The number of people condemned at the Old Bailey, London, between 1749 and 1771 was 1,121 of whom 678 were executed and 443 pardoned. From 1718, as an alternative punishment, some of the convicted prisoners were transported for life to the American colonies, particularly Maryland, to work on the plantations there. As a result of the American War of Independence, it was no longer possible to send them to America. From 1776 many convicts were held in hulks, former warships moored near dockyards and arsenals where the prisoners worked.

The punishment for less serious crimes—such as using profane language or not attending church—was fines, whipping, the pillory or the stocks. Men or women who got into debt—even though it was only for a few shillings—could be sent to prison. Prisons were then run by gaolers for their own personal profit; they could make a charge for admitting a debtor, for releasing him, and were even licensed to sell beer and sometimes wine to those prisoners who could afford to buy it. Men and women debtors, felons and petty offenders, were all crowded together into the prisons, where hundreds died of smallpox, and gaol (or typhus) fever.

In 1774 some improvement was made in prison conditions, as a result of the efforts of that remarkable reformer, John Howard. As Sheriff of the County of Bedford in 1773, he had come to learn of 'the distress of prisoners' and asked the local bench of magistrates to pay the gaoler a salary, so that he would no longer have to ill-treat those prisoners who could not afford to pay his fees. The magistrates agreed to do so, if Howard could show that other counties did the same.

A Perspective View of the Execution of Lord Ferrers at TYBURN May 5. 1760. for the Murder of his Steward

Printed for Robt. Wilkinson, 58 Cornhill.

Execution of Lord Ferrers.
*In 1760 Lord Ferrers was hanged
at Tyburn for murdering his
steward.*

He went first to a few nearby counties and finding the conditions in their prisons just as shocking decided to extend his investigations to all the county gaols of England, and then to those on the Continent. His reports to the House of Commons and his books made people aware of the need for reform. He found that in one case a weaver had been sent to prison for a debt of 10s. 2d., and was charged 10s. 6d. by the gaoler for being brought to the gaol, which was only seven miles away. His visits to prisons were made at great danger to his own health; most people then did not dare to put a foot inside a prison for fear of catching gaol fever. He himself died of fever in Russia in 1790.

There were no policemen to maintain public order and to prevent crime, even in the most populous city of London. Each parish had only an elected or appointed constable, and sometimes night watchmen. It was up to each person to provide for his own protection. Owners of the London pleasure parks, which were patronised mainly by the middle classes and the gentry, had to provide their own security guards if they did not want their customers to be deterred from visiting them at night. Thomas Keyse, proprietor of the Bermondsey Spa Gardens, made a special point in his newspaper advertisements of the fact that 'for the security of the public the road (from the gardens to London Bridge) is lighted and watched by patrols every night, at the sole expense of the proprietor'.

Around the middle of the eighteenth century, the writer Henry Fielding and his half-brother, Sir John, became magistrates at Bow Street. They formed a volunteer band of householders—the famous Bow Street runners—to protect property and to maintain public law and order. In 1805 Sir Richard Ford, who was then the chief magistrate at Bow Street, started a horse patrol on the main roads leading to the metropolis to guard travellers against highwaymen.

Because of the lack of police and the great amount of poverty, crime was common in the eighteenth century. And so were riots, particularly when food prices were high. Under the Riot Act of 1714, a magistrate or mayor could order a crowd to disperse by reading the Riot Act. The penalty for disobeying this order was transportation or death. But if the crowd refused to disperse, there was nothing the authorities could do, until the military arrived. Although the soldiers usually obeyed their officers, it was not unknown for them to take the rioters' side. This was understandable, for their lot was even harder than that of the rioters.

For the slightest act of disobedience the soldier could be flogged. In the 1770s their pay was only just over £8 a year and out of this they had, in most regiments, to buy their uniform, because their colonel wanted his troops to be the smartest in the army. Few soldiers protested officially as their protests would have been ignored, or been instantly punished by a flogging; and even fewer protested publicly because they were too illiterate to do so. One exception was a soldier from a lower middle-class family who pub-

The Watchhouse.
Rowlandson's impression of night watchmen.

The Battle of Albuera.
*An artist's impression of the
battlefields in the Peninsular War*

lished a journal in 1770. He had first been apprenticed to 'an agreeable business' but being 'of a rambling disposition' he ran away at the age of 15 to enlist in the 68th Regiment of Foot, commanded by General Lambton. He wrote: 'Besides the grievous acts of oppression exercised on the soldiery in general, their pay, to live on, does not exceed one shilling and seven pence half-penny per week, clear of all deductions. . . . Within twenty years the soldier was never required to appear in anything beyond the usual allowance of the government; but now the scene is quite altered, you cannot appear without white stockings, leather breeches, short gaiters, hair powdered and several other very unnecessary articles of apparel, too tedious to be mentioned.'

It was these conditions which made many recruits decide to serve with the East India Company rather than the Army. The company offered much higher rates of pay. But, as the anonymous soldier pointed out, there was a snag in that, too. Most of the recruits died abroad and few ever returned to enjoy the fruits of their service.

A 'Peeler', 1837.
The new police soon became a familiar sight in the streets of London.

The Years of Growth

Great reforms were made during this period. The number of offences punishable by death was drastically reduced; police forces were started; and conditions in both the prisons and the army were improved.

At the beginning of the nineteenth century, Sir Samuel Romilly had succeeded, against considerable opposition, in getting a Bill passed which abolished the death penalty for the crime of picking pockets of goods to the value of a shilling. But there were still over 200 crimes for which the death penalty could be imposed, including the 'offence' of injuring Westminster Bridge. By 1832 it was no longer a capital offence to steal a sheep, or to break into a house. Six years later these 200 capital offences had been reduced to a basic two—murder and attempted murder. In spite of this, many people still held that 'crime' should be countered with the severest penalties. In September, 1828, the *Morning Chronicle* reported a case at the Middlesex Sessions in which a number of boys were accused of stealing. The offence of one 'little hungry-looking boy', aged about 12, was to have stolen two buns and eight biscuits. The chairman of the bench said that the only effective way of stopping such 'crime' was transportation. 'Whipping used to make some impression upon them,' he went on, 'but now they quite disregard it. However, I'll give these boys another chance —let them be confined for three months and be *twice* well whipped.'

Opposition to the creation of a police force was as great as it was to the reduction of severe punishments. Critics felt that a police force, like a standing army, would result in a loss of personal liberty. In the 1820s, the main police forces in London, apart from the parish constables and night watchmen, were still the horse patrol, the 82 members of the Bow Street night foot patrol and the 24 members of the day foot patrol. The day patrol wore scarlet waistcoats, blue coats and Wellington boots. The minimum height was 5 feet 5 inches (people were much

The Treadmill.
*A common means of
punishment in nineteenth
century gaols.*

shorter then on average than they are now). Even though some of the patrols carried pistols, in addition to their truncheons, the force was completely inadequate, as there were 10,000 streets to patrol and protect.

In 1829, largely as a result of the efforts of Sir Robert Peel, the Metropolitan Police was formed in London. In September of that year, the first 1,000 of the Metropolitan Police, in their blue tailcoats and top hats, started to patrol the London streets. The force was soon trebled in size.

As the crime rate in London started to fall, other big cities established their own forces. But there were still many country areas without a police force. It was not until the Police Act of 1856 was passed that magistrates were required to establish police forces in all areas which still lacked one.

In spite of some reforms, conditions in the prisons were still extremely bad. Short-term prisoners were kept in the hulks, of which there were 10 in 1826, containing between 3,000 and 4,000 prisoners. Those sentenced to 14 years or more were transported to Australia, instead of to America. Before being sent overseas, criminals were held in prison. It was amongst these women that a Quaker, Elizabeth Fry, started her work in Newgate Prison in 1813. She supplied the women with decent clothes and improved the conditions on ships taking convicts to Australia. She opened a school in the prison, read the Bible to the women prisoners, and got them to do useful work, such as knitting.

Owing to pressure from Australian settlers, transportation to Australia was stopped in the 1840s, though it went on for a few more years to Tasmania. Because convicts could no longer be disposed of in this way, it became necessary to provide more prisons in England. In 1842 the 'model' prison of Pentonville was opened, and within six years 54 other prisons, with accommodation for 11,000 prisoners, were built on the same plan.

The prisons were run on two principles—separate confinement and hard labour. The first required the isolation of the prisoner in his own cell and the second meant fatiguing work, breaking stones and working on the treadmill. In 1863 a Committee of the House of Lords found in favour of this system, based on 'hard labour, hard fare and a hard bed'. When the county gaols were taken over by a Board of Prison Commissioners 14 years later, these principles were applied uniformly to all prisons. There was, however, one

reform at least and that was the end of public executions in the 1860s.

During this period, reforms were made in the British Army. Life in the Army was brutal in war and not much better in times of peace. The last great campaigns fought by the Army had been during the Peninsular War and at Waterloo. All the horrors of the Peninsular campaigns were vividly described by one soldier who wrote of the battlefield of Vimeiro: 'I saw one man faint with loss of blood, staggering along and turned to assist him. He was severely wounded in the head, his face being completely encrusted with blood which had flowed during the night and had now dried. One eyeball was knocked out of the socket and hung down upon his cheek.'

But the memories of those campaigns receded as the Army settled down to its peace-

A Ward at Scutari.
Florence Nightingale ministering to the wounded during the Crimean War.

time existence, fighting no major wars and only some engagements in India and other colonies. Low pay, brutal floggings for the smallest offence, and bad living conditions, made the Army unattractive for any but the most destitute of men. In 1851 it was found that 37 per cent of the men in the ranks were Irish. They had joined the Army to escape the even worse consequences of the potato famine in Ireland.

It was the shock of defeats and disasters in the Crimean War which was to open the eyes of the public—and some of the Army Officers themselves—to the need for reforms. Writing in 1855, one lieutenant-colonel said: 'The equipment and organisation of our army are defective. . . . Our experience had been dearly bought. . . . It is written alas! in the ravines before Sebastopol; it is recorded in the graveyards of Scutari.' He went on to say: 'The army, as at present paid and treated is little more than a refuge for the destitute youth of the United Kingdom. And less a refuge, unfortunately than a trap. . . .' The promise of a bounty paid in gold led many youths to join up, only to find that most of it would be absorbed by buying their kit which cost £3 13s. 1d. Their pay of 1s. a day was diminished by stoppages for pipe-clay, blacking, hair-cutting, barrack-damages and other charges. One of his main proposals for reform was that their pay should be increased to 1s. 6d. a day.

The victories of the Prussian armies on the Continent in 1866 and 1870 finally convinced the English that their army must be completely reformed. Between 1868 and 1874, short-service engagements were introduced, the purchase of commissions was abolished, a month's leave was given to well-behaved soldiers in the winter and flogging was stopped in times of peace.

Modern Times

During the modern period, criminals have received far more sympathy and understanding than they ever did in the past. In 1895 a committee, presided over by Gladstone, reported on the prison system. It found that the methods of separating prisoners from each other and making them do arduous and pointless work had failed. Fear of prison had not deterred people from committing crimes, neither had experience of it prevented criminals from continuing in their old ways. In fact, the degradation of prison life meant that many prisoners had become even more brutalised and embittered by the time they were released.

The committee called for a new approach towards the criminal. Prison should still act as a deterrent, but at the same time 'treatment should be effectually designed to maintain, stimulate, or awaken the higher susceptibilities of prisoners and to turn them out of prison better men and women, physically and morally, than when they came in'. These two aims of punishment and reform were difficult to reconcile, and little effort was made to do so before the First World War.

Instead, an attempt was made to keep as many offenders as possible out of prison altogether, unless it appeared absolutely necessary that they should go there. One of the biggest aids towards this end was the setting up of the probation service. Towards the end of the nineteenth century, a number of voluntary societies had appointed missionaries at magistrates' courts. They tried to help offenders who had been given a conditional discharge. Many magistrates kept in close contact with these court missionaries.

Their work was encouraged when a law was passed in 1887 allowing first offenders, found guilty of a crime which could be punished with not more than two years' imprisonment, to be released 'on probation of good conduct'. Twenty years later, in 1907, another law allowed justices to appoint probation officers if they wished to do so. (In

1925, it was made compulsory.) Although the probation service has usually been understaffed and underpaid, it has had considerable success in keeping a number of first offenders from committing subsequent crimes.

These laws were just two of the many which were passed before the First World War with the aim of keeping as many offenders as possible out of prison. In 1908 a new law sought to keep young people under 21 out of prison unless there was no other appropriate method of dealing with them. Under this law, the Borstal system of training became a recognised part of the penal code. (The first Borstal had been set up at Borstal Prison near Rochester, Kent, in 1902.) In 1908, also, another act set up special juvenile courts for children under 16 (later 17). And in 1914 a Criminal Justice Act required magistrates to allow people time in which to pay fines as an alternative to imprisonment, unless there was some good reason for their not doing so.

The debate over whether prison should be a place of punishment or of reform continued after the First World War, as it has done to the present time. But in 1948 a Criminal Justice Act lessened some of the severities of prison life by abolishing the sentences of hard labour and penal servitude and came down more heavily upon the side of reform. 'The purposes of training and treatment of convicted prisoners shall be to establish in them the will to lead a good and useful life on discharge and fit them to do so.' Towards this end, efforts have been made in some prisons to provide work which is likely to help prisoners to earn their own living after release and also, less commonly, to provide some technical training. Some 'open' prisons have also been built for selected offenders. On the whole, people are no longer sent to prison only *for* punishment but *as* a punishment. But many vestiges of the older system of separation—like the cells—still remain.

At the same time as society has moderated its attitude towards the individual offender, so that physical cruelty is no longer practised

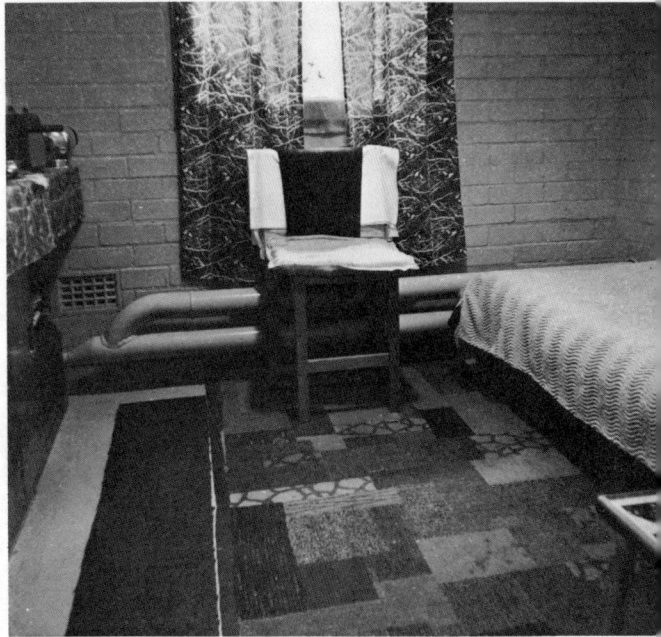

Maximum Security Prison.
A cell at Blundeston Prison, Lowestoft, Suffolk, 1963.

upon him as it once was, new weapons have enabled man to practise mass destruction on a scale which has never been known before.

It was the First World War that marked the turning point. A slight foretaste of modern developments was provided by the Boer War of 1899–1902. Casualties on the British side were not particularly high. Out of total forces of nearly half a million men in all, only 5,774 were killed. Indeed far more British soldiers—over 16,000—were killed by fever and other diseases than by fighting. The Boer losses were much heavier proportionately, both among fighting men, of whom about 4,000 died, and civilians. About 4,000 Boer women and 16,000 children died from disease in what the British called blockhouses and the Boers called concentration camps. They had been opened for refugees from the farmsteads destroyed in the 'scorched earth' policy adopted during the war. But when the camps were first opened, overcrowding, insufficient medical care and inadequate rations took their toll among inmates, whose number rose eventually to nearly 200,000. Mounting public criticism in Britain and

First World War.
*A graphic view of the desolate
loneliness of war.*

greater experience of running the camps caused the death rate to fall considerably before the end of the war.

The war had started with a series of disastrous defeats for the British, and even when these had ended, the Boers adopted guerrilla tactics which continued to harass the British troops. The war had an enormous impact on British public opinion. The rejection of 40 per cent of recruits on medical grounds revealed the widespread extent of poverty at home. The initial series of defeats tarnished the image of a Great Britain. Different people drew different conclusions.

Some people, like Mrs. Arthur Phillp, put the troubles down to lack of 'obedience, self-discipline and unselfishness in the home'.

She formed a Ministering Children's League to encourage these virtues. She was one of the contributors to a book called *Essays on Duty and Discipline* published in 1910. The book had a great vogue and ran through five editions in 13 months. In one of the essays, Mrs. Phillp wrote: 'The diminishing birth-rate shows that women are showing the "white feather", that they prefer amusements, sports and idleness to the sweet toils and endless duties of motherhood. Men show the spirit which, to our sorrow and surprise, made Englishmen surrender so often in the Boer War and soldiers throw down their arms. . . .'

There were many people who thought that conscription should be introduced. Mrs.

Phillp was amongst them. 'Undoubtedly,' she wrote, 'one great indirect gain to our nation if a year or two's compulsory military service comes into the life of all our boys will be the training in habits of respect and obedience.' Conscription was not introduced. Instead, the Army was reorganised by Lord Haldane and a Territorial Army was formed. The British Expeditionary Force which went to France in August, 1914, was efficient and highly trained.

The First World War, between the Allied powers and Germany and the central powers, was largely a static war. For much of the time the armies in their trenches faced each other across a small strip of mud and devastation—no-man's-land. Sniping and raids went on all the time. In the big battles there was a reckless expenditure of human lives. Casualties were very high. In all, the total number of troops killed on both sides was about 10 million, of whom over 1 million came from the British Empire. Britain relied upon its regular Army and Territorials until 1916, when conscription was introduced.

In the Second World War, the world total of those killed and missing was even higher than in the previous war. In all, it was estimated to exceed 15 million. But the losses of the British Commonwealth were lower than in the First World War—just over half a million.

For the first time, however, the number of civilians killed was very great. The aeroplane brought war into the homes of almost all contesting countries. Many thousands of civilians were killed and injured in air raids and V1 and V2 rocket attacks on Britain. In Europe, about 6 million people died in German concentration camps. And on August 6, 1945, a new era in mass destruction was opened when the first atomic bomb was dropped on Hiroshima in Japan. A second bomb was dropped on Nagasaki three days later. Mankind had entered the atomic age.

Attitudes towards the individual offender against society's laws have altered greatly in the last two centuries. In the eighteenth century they were hurled into a dark, insanitary gaol, where few but the bravest would ever visit them, or transported far overseas. Often, the main cause of their offence had been nothing but poverty. There is now a much more sympathetic attitude towards the criminal, both officially and publicly. But there is still a large body of public opinion which feels that attitudes have swung too much the other way, and that the treatment of criminals is more sympathetic than it should be. The nature of criminality is still not fully understood: certainly, affluence has not brought about the expected diminution in crime.

At the same time as the official attitude towards the individual criminal has softened, and punishments of them are less cruel than they once were, science has provided the means of mass destruction which man has never possessed before. Formerly, disasters were caused by natural means—plagues, earthquakes and floods; now man himself, armed with atomic weapons, possesses the ability to cause widespread devastation on a much vaster scale. Only two atomic bombs have ever been dropped. For the last 20 years an uneasy peace has been preserved in Europe at least by the balance of 'nuclear terror'. Some people maintain that while weapons of mass destruction still exist, it is likely that they will eventually be used. Disarmament is still as far off as ever, but one encouraging fact is that many statesmen, scientists and academics are far more conscious of the dangers of war and the need to avoid it than they ever have been in the past.

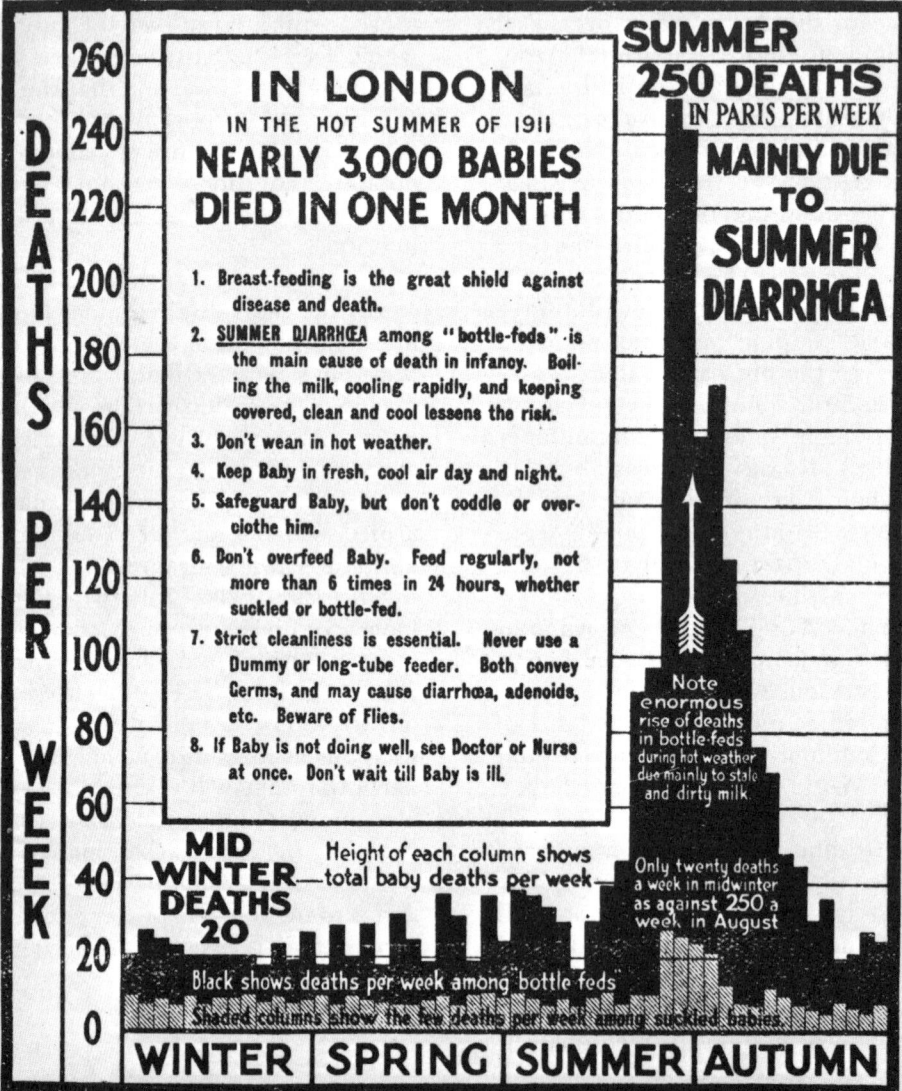

'Save the Babies'. *A warning poster published in 1918 to remind mothers of the danger of summer illnesses amongst babies.*

5. SICKNESS AND MOURNING

The Georgian Age

Throughout the whole period, and indeed beyond, it was generally believed that diseases were caused by impurities in the atmosphere, or the 'foulness of the air'. This belief was not entirely surprising, for in London and the other major cities, bad smells were just as numerous as diseases. The people rarely washed either themselves or their clothes. There was virtually no sanitation, only a privy whose contents were occasionally tipped into the streets, or into a convenient stream, or on to the public refuse heap. In Barnard Castle, Co. Durham, for example, weavers and other labourers dwelt in confined courts and alleys, with sometimes as many as 50 people living together in one house. Even by the end of the period, there was only one privy at the most, and sometimes none at all, to each yard (or onset, as it was called there), which contained five or six houses, accommodating as many as 200 or 300 people.

Most of the streets were narrow—often less than 6 feet wide—and unpaved. In Manchester, at the end of the period many streets were still 'so deep in mire or so full of hollows and refuse' that no cart could use them. The streets were 'worn into deep ruts and holes, in which the water constantly stagnates and are so covered with refuse and other matter as to be almost impassable from depth of mud, and intolerable from stench'. The streets were the general rubbish bins of the residents. Into them, the butchers, tanners, sausage makers and other tradesmen threw all their waste material, while the residents added their slops and garbage, leaving it to rot and moulder in the unstirring air. Or, if there were a stream nearby they would tip all their refuse into that, even though this same stream, or the river into which it flowed, was probably the main source of water for the inhabitants.

All the cities were full of 'privies in the most disgusting state of filth, open cesspools, obstructed drains, ditches full of stagnant water, dunghills, and pigsties' with many people living 10 to a room, often in a cellar liable to flooding, and sometimes with their pigs, chickens, and even horses or cows sharing the same room with them.

In the country, conditions were scarcely any better. In Bedford, for example, as late as 1840, it was found that very few cottages had privies that could be used. 'Contiguous to almost every door a dung heap was raised.' Scarcely any of the cottages had a pantry; the food was kept in the one bedroom in which the whole family often slept together.

Richer people provided what personal protection they could against the foul stench of the towns. John Howard, on his prison tours, hoped to guard himself against gaol fever and smallpox by 'smelling to vinegar' and changing his clothes after each visit. But the diseases that these insanitary conditions bred—typhus, typhoid, dysentry, cholera and smallpox—could not be controlled until there was more knowledge of their cause and better living conditions in the towns. Some improvements in both spheres were to be made during this period.

In London and many other large cities, a start was made on paving and draining the roads. These measures were initially taken not so much to improve the health of the inhabitants, but to speed up the traffic in the cities. In 1710 there were 800 hackney-coaches, and 200 sedan chairs, plying for hire in London, in addition to the stage-coaches, wagons, carts, pack-horses and the private coaches of the rich. In the narrow streets, there were often traffic jams when a coach overturned or became stuck in the rutted, muddy surface of the road.

It was to prevent such delays and to give passengers a smoother ride that the streets began to be paved and drained from about the middle of the eighteenth century. It was noticed, however, that where this was done the health of the inhabitants was also improved. It was particularly noticeable in Portsmouth. The town, which was built upon marshy ground, was paved in 1769; this brought an end to 'the intermittent fever' which had formerly prevailed there.

Fryingpan Alley, Clerkenwell.
*Water still had to be obtained
from the public pump.*

But the inhabitants of nearby Hilsea continued to suffer from this disorder until their streets were paved, too, in 1793.

In addition to this improvement in public health, there were also some improvements in medicine, particularly in the provision of hospitals. Formerly, the only hospitals had been those which had once been attached to religious houses—like St. Bartholomew's in London—or the infirmaries attached to poorhouses set up under the Elizabethan Poor Law.

Between 1720 and 1752 five major hospitals were founded in London, including the Westminster, Guy's and the Middlesex. Many hospitals were built in the provinces, too, the first being the County Hospital at Winchester in 1736. These voluntary hospitals were financed by rich individuals and by subscriptions from the middle classes and were intended for the treatment of the sick poor. Some medical improvements were made, particularly in midwifery. There was a slight improvement in hygiene, with some hospitals shutting wards for certain periods of the year. But with no knowledge of anti-

St Bartholomew's Hospital.
*Nursing staff at work in the
mid-nineteenth century.*

The Cow Pock — or — the Wonderful Effects of the New Inoculation! — Vide the Publications of ye Anti-Vaccine Society

'The Cow Pock'.
A cartoonist's view of some of the side-effects of vaccination.

septic precautions, the wards remained infected with the diseases of previous patients, while the wooden beds, in which two patients commonly slept together, were infested with bugs. In 1764 iron bedsteads were provided in one ward of St. Thomas's Hospital, London, and in the rest of the wards a few years later. Bart's did not have them until 1815.

Some attempt was also made to segregate fever patients from others. The majority of hospitals started in the eighteenth century were general hospitals, but in 1802 the London Fever Hospital was opened. Other specialised hospitals followed, including Moorfields Eye Hospital in 1805 and the Royal Hospital for Diseases of the Chest in 1814.

But medical knowledge remained sketchy; and surgery was painful. There were no anaesthetics or antiseptic precautions. Before an operation the patient might be given the juice of the poppy or of hemp to relieve pain. More often he was simply given a very strong drink of brandy and held down by three or four strong men while the surgeon did his work as quickly as he could. The instruments were not sterilised and the surgeon and his assistants wore greasy bloodstained clothes. Medical care consisted largely of bleeding the patient; making him sick; and then giving him purgatives.

Amongst the most pitiful patients were the insane, confined in Bethlehem Hospital, or Bedlam as it was known. As late as 1815 when a Select Committee of the House of Commons made an investigation into the hospital, some patients were still secured in their bed by a collar round their neck, a chain round their ankles and were also completely enclosed in an iron cage which left only their arms free to move. To visit Bedlam was a favourite Sunday sport for many people. A penny or twopence was charged for admission. This practice was not stopped until 1770.

In such conditions it was not surprising that funerals were very frequent.

The rich had a respectable funeral. As the mourners left the house, a servant would present them with a sprig of rosemary which they threw into the grave. But in times of plague, which were common then, shallow pits were dug into which the dead, both rich and poor, were unceremoniously tipped. In some parts of the country, these mass graves were used even in normal times for paupers and all who could not afford to pay for a respectable burial. In Manchester, these pits were known as Poor's Holes. But practice varied. In other parts of the country, even paupers were given a decent burial. One parish paid for the church bell to be tolled, while another provided drink and biscuits for the bearers.

The Years of Growth

People had come to dread the shame of a pauper's funeral. A middle-class funeral, with its 20 bearers and stave-bearers dressed in black, and beplumed horses pulling the funeral coach containing the lead coffin, cost £50 to £70 in the 1840s. It was, therefore, quite beyond the means of ordinary folk. But they wanted a decent elm coffin, bearers and at least five pairs of mourners for their funeral, which cost about £4.

For this, they were prepared to save. In Preston, Lancs, in 1840 there were six flourishing burial societies with nearly 30,000 members, who paid from $\frac{1}{2}d$. to 2d. a week so that they could have a decent funeral. These clubs provided good business for the undertakers and for the pubs in which the headquarters of the Societies were usually to be found. But many people could not afford even these small weekly payments.

Nevertheless, 'the desire to secure respectful interment of themselves and their relatives is, perhaps, the strongest and most widely-diffused feeling amongst the labouring classes of the population', wrote Sir Edwin Chadwick in 1843 in his report on burials in towns. This simple desire—as his report clearly showed—resulted in a great danger to public health.

In the poorest areas of the towns, the funeral was delayed while the family tried to raise the necessary £4, or to get credit from the undertaker. Frequently, all members of the family, sometimes as many as 10 of them, all lived together in one room. Until the money could be found, the corpse stayed with them. Sometimes it occupied the only bed. Or it lay, stretched out upon two chairs, to be 'pulled about by the children and made to serve as a resting place for any article that is in the way', as one clergyman of a 'wretchedly crowded parish' testified.

London Main Drainage. *Works such as these made the capital a more hygienic place to live in.*

LONDON MAIN DRAINAGE.

WORKS AT BARKING CREEK OUTFALL.

PUMPING-STATION AT DEPTFORD CREEK.

DRIVING A TUNNEL AT PECKHAM.

BOTTOM OF A SHAFT IN THE SOUTHERN HIGH-LEVEL SEWER AT PECKHAM.

Usually, it lay there for five days at least, and sometimes as many as 12—with all the consequent dangers to the health of the surviving members of the family.

The overcrowded graveyards in the towns were an equal source of danger. Some grave-diggers actually died while working in them, but the biggest danger was hidden. The graveyards polluted the neighbouring wells, from which the inhabitants drew their drinking water. In his report, Chadwick recommended that burial in the town churchyards should be stopped and that national cemeteries should be opened in their place. In fact a cemetery at Kensal Green had been established by private enterprise in 1832. In the 1850s, with a very few exceptions, the London churchyards were closed for burials, and the provision of cemeteries started to become general.

Chadwick's other great report on the 'sanitary state of the labouring population of Great Britain', published in 1842, was equally outspoken. The conclusion he came to was that 'the annual loss of life from filth and bad ventilation are greater than the loss from death or wounds in any wars in which the country has been engaged in modern times'. He urged that there should be better sanitation and drainage, pure water supplies, street cleaning and collection of all household refuse. All of these measures were most urgently needed. A report on Leeds, published in 1840, revealed that 'for three streets in the Bank, containing 100 dwellings, and a population of 452 persons, there are but two small offices, neither of which is fit for use; one street being wholly destitute of such provision. . . . If there be neither sewerage, drainage, nor out-offices, how can the inhabitants of the parts of the town accommodate themselves, and how do they get rid of their refuse? The answer is that in a great measure the adult population use the offices of their respective places of employment, and that all the refuse of their dwellings is thrown into the street, where pools of water accumulate and stagnate . . . or sump holes are used for absorbing it.'

To remedy these conditions, the first Public Health Act was passed in 1848, which allowed cities to set up local boards to deal with matters affecting health. A few cities were already taking action. Manchester was building sewers by the time the Act was passed and in 1848 started to construct the first large water reservoir in the country.

But progress in providing sanitation was very slow and varied greatly from one part of the country to another. The first water closet had been designed by Sir John Harington in the sixteenth century and the first modern w.c. was patented by Joseph Bramah in 1778. But it was not until the 1830s that they started to be installed and then only in houses in 'the wealthy or newly-built districts'. Main sewerage, in any case, was still not available even in many of the best parts of the town. In Red Lion Square and Bedford Row, London, cesspools were still in use up to 1854; the contents soaked away into the ground below the house, or were carried out in buckets through the house when the cesspool became overfull. By 1865 the main sewers in London had all been completed, but in the same year many towns, such as Widnes, Lancashire, with its population of 10,000, had no public sewers at all. Even in London in the 1880s there were still whole areas where the outside closets were blocked or had been overflowing for months.

There was just as great a lack of pure water supplies as there was of sanitation. For their water, the poor relied mainly on pumps and wells, and if these were far off they would get it from any muddy stream nearby. Of 50 large towns examined in 1842 only six had good water supplies; in 31 they were inadequate or impure. It was not until the 1860s that a Royal Commission declared that the supply of pure water was necessary for 'civilised social life' and not until much later than clean, fresh water was brought within the reach of everyone.

Meanwhile, some local councils and some private individuals tried to remedy these defects. In 1859 the Metropolitan Free Drinking Fountain Association was founded by Samuel Gurney, M.P., a nephew of Elizabeth Fry. The first fountain was erected in the same year on the wall of St. Sepulchre's Church, Snow Hill, and by 1866 there were 110 fountains scattered about London. In that year, troughs for dogs were added to a number of them. The organisation was already providing drinking troughs for cattle and horses and in 1867 it changed its name to the present one—The Metropolitan Drinking Fountain and Cattle Trough Association.

During this period too there were enormous advances in medical care. The death rate in some major operations, such as amputation of a limb, was still very high at the beginning of the period. Two out of three patients died. Without anaesthetics, it was necessary for the surgeon to work very quickly. It was said of the surgeon Robert Liston that 'the gleam of his knife was followed so instantaneously by the sound of sawing as to make the two actions appear almost simultaneous'. It was Liston who performed the first operation with an anaesthetic in Great Britain—at University College Hospital, London, in 1846. The

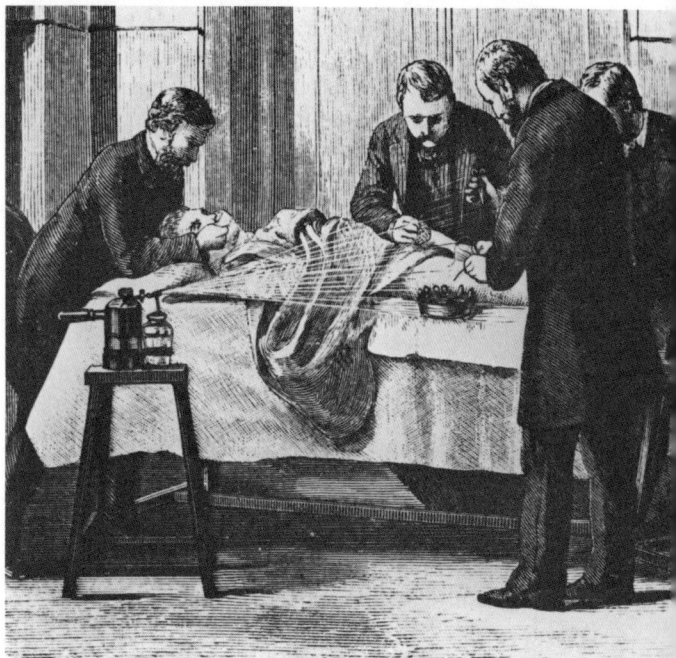

An Operation.
The early days of antiseptic surgery under chloroform.

An Operation.
The interior of a Barber-Surgeon's shop.

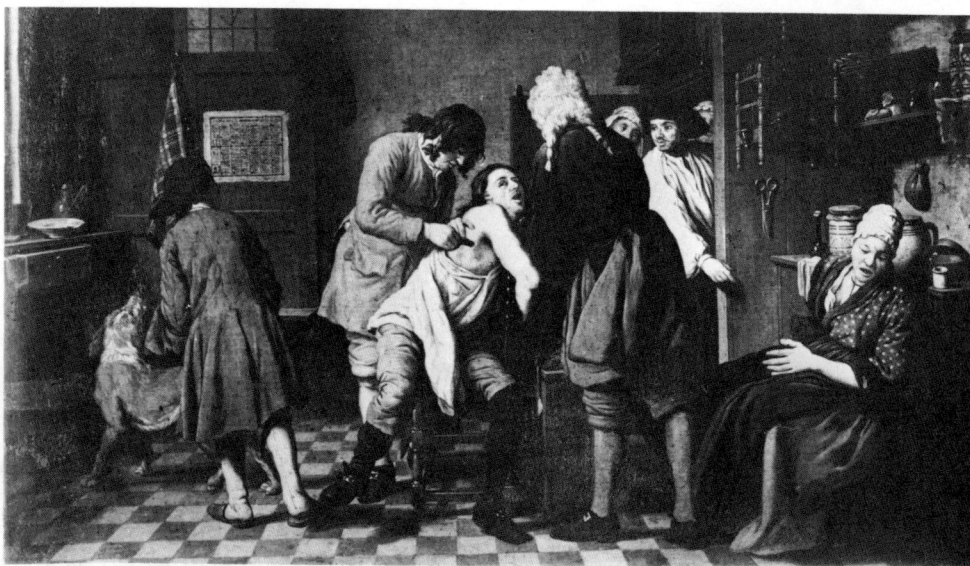

following year, Sir James Simpson published a pamphlet about the use of chloroform, instead of ether, as an anaesthetic and within a few years it was in widespread use. The development of antiseptic surgery had to await the researches of Joseph Lister, who published two articles on the subject in the medical journal, the *Lancet*, in 1867.

The work and status of nurses was completely revolutionised by Florence Nightingale. Formerly, most nurses had been underpaid, uneducated and performed mainly a housemaid's work. Florence Nightingale changed all that. In 1860 the Florence Nightingale Training School was opened at St. Thomas's Hospital—with 15 students dressed in their uniforms of long brown dresses, and white aprons and caps. In spite of some doctors' opposition, nursing was to become a career in its own right, with educated, trained nurses no longer responsible only to doctors, but also to their own matrons.

For all these reasons the number of epidemics declined. There had been serious outbreaks of cholera in London in 1831, 1848–9 and 1865–6. After 1866 there was no serious epidemic. Deaths from typhoid, typhus and scarlet fever all started to decline after 1880. People lived longer and even those who became ill had a better change of surviving.

Modern Times

One of the biggest changes in modern times has been in the provision of comprehensive social security by the State. Although national health insurance schemes are new, man's need for some form of insurance in times of illness and sickness is not. Voluntary schemes run by friendly societies have existed from at least the seventeenth century. There was an enormous growth in their number and extent in the nineteenth century, when some of the biggest friendly societies were formed. The Manchester Unity of Oddfellows was founded in 1810, and the Ancient Order of Foresters in 1834. These were both nation-wide organisations with branches in different parts of the country.

In the nineteenth century there were also many smaller friendly societies, usually with their headquarters in a public house. One of these was the Admiral Nelson Society, which used to meet in the Saddle Inn, Briggate, Leeds. The members had to be between 16 and 32, in perfect health and 'not liable to be disordered at particular seasons of the year . . . nor a soldier, sea-faring man, miner, delver, chimney sweeper, or dipper in the potteries'. Each member had to pay a contribution of 3s. 9d. a quarter. They received 9s. a week when they were prevented from working by sickness or injury, unless it had been caused by 'intoxication, fighting, wrestling, leaping, racing or illegal practices'. The benefit was reduced to 2s. 6d. a week after a year. There was also a burial grant of £7 and a pension of 2s. 6d. a week at the age of 70.

The trouble with many of these friendly societies was that, like the Admiral Nelson, they excluded people in the particularly dangerous occupations who were most in need of protection and security. Furthermore, the contributions were too high for many workers. The most they could afford to join was a burial club—and some of them could not afford even that.

The origins of the modern system of medical care and social security go back only to

1912 when a National Health Insurance scheme came into operation. Under this scheme, all workers who earned less than £3 a week—the mass of the working classes —had to pay in 4d. a week towards the cost of the scheme, while their employers contributed 3d. and the State 2d. Contributors could obtain the services of a 'panel' doctor in case of need, and if they were unable to work they received 10s. a week sickness benefit. But the scheme did not cover the worker's wife or his children. Hospital treatment was still provided by the voluntary hospitals, the poor law institutions or new municipal hospitals. These were still used mainly by the working class until the First World War. Previously the middle and upper classes had been nursed at home or in expensive private nursing homes. But during the First World War many wounded soldiers of the middle classes were nursed back to health in ordinary hospitals. Some voluntary hospitals also started to provide private beds for those who could afford to pay.

In 1948 the National Health Service was started, to promote, in the words of the Act, 'a comprehensive health service designed to secure improvement in the physical and mental health of the people . . . and the prevention, diagnosis and treatment of illness'. Practically all hospitals came under Government control. The majority of doctors, dentists and opticians also made their services available to National Health patients.

Just before this, a National Insurance scheme had been started. Based on the Beveridge Report of 1942, it provided a whole range of benefits, not only for medical care, but also for unemployment, retirement and death. Between them, these two schemes have taken much of the anxiety out of illness —as far as the financial aspect is concerned —and provided for the majority of people security such as they had never known before.

Even just before the last war, there were many people who could not afford to visit an optician. Instead, they went to Woolworth's. Most of these stores had a large display of

spectacles of all kinds, and a sight-testing card for a do-it-yourself prescription. Other people used large magnifying glasses for reading. Many people's teeth—particularly those of children—were in a shocking state. Dental decay was one of the main reasons for the rejection of so many recruits during the Boer War.

Toothbrushes and toothpowders had been used by the middle classes since the beginning of the nineteenth century, but at the beginning of the twentieth century vast numbers of people still never cleaned their teeth at all. Even if they had done so, their diet was so deficient in bone-forming foods that their teeth would probably have rotted anyway.

Another cause of dental decay were the working conditions in some industries. When R. H. Sherard visited the chemical workers of Widnes in 1897 he found that nearly all of them had bad teeth. Nevertheless, they roared with laughter at the joke about the chemical worker who had to pay a man 'to masticate his food for him. This last joke tickled them specially, and they grinned with their black gums.'

One result of this bad diet and lack of proper dental care was the great increase in the use of dentures, or false teeth. These were called 'patent masticators' when they were first produced. Many ordinary people could not afford to go to a dentist for them, and bought a second-hand pair from a junk shop instead. This went on until the beginning of the Second World War.

In modern times there has been enormous progress in medicine and surgery. X-rays were discovered in 1895 and some of the uses of penicillin in 1928, to mention but two of the many advances. Greater medical knowledge and skill combined with improved understanding of nutrition are mainly responsible for the fact that a boy born today can expect to live 16 years longer and a girl nearly 19 years longer than one born 50 years ago.

Sanitation and water supplies continued to improve in the towns. Toilet paper—

originally known as 'curl paper' by genteel ladies—had already been in use before the modern period opened. The first perforated rolls of toilet paper were introduced in the 1880s and interleaved paper about 10 years later. It remained a luxury for many of the working class, and right up to the Second World War and beyond many of them used squares cut from newspapers instead. Modern sanitation and water supplies are still not available in some of the remote parts of the country.

There has been an equally big change in funeral customs. By the beginning of the twentieth century the middle class had given up the habit of wearing hatbands and cloaks

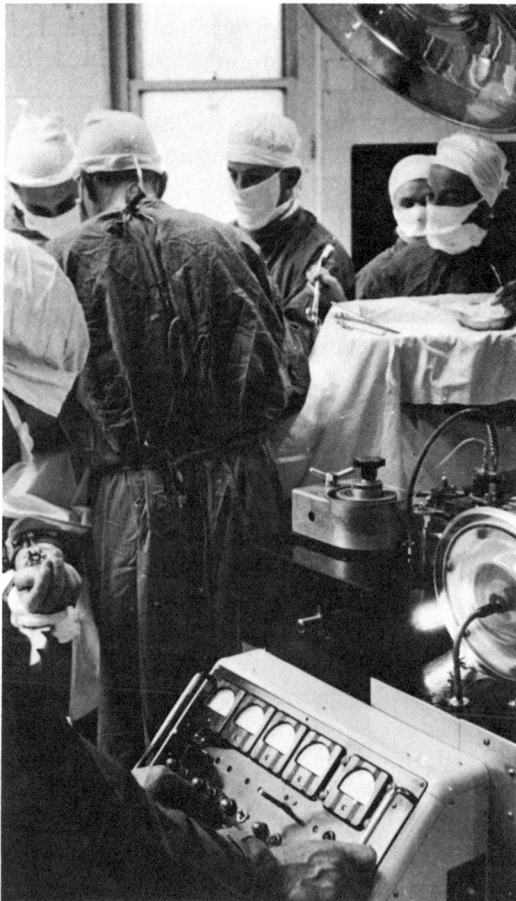

Heart and lung machine.
In use at Hammersmith Hospital.

at funerals. It was no longer common for the family to go into full mourning when someone died. Instead, they wore a band of black cloth round their left sleeve. Even that custom has now virtually died out. But there was an even bigger change in the method of disposing of the dead.

A Cremation Society had been formed in 1874 by Sir Henry Thompson, surgeon to Queen Victoria, and four years later a crematorium was built on a site at Woking, Surrey. It was not used immediately, however, because there was still great opposition from the Home Office towards cremation and some doubts as to its legality. But after a celebrated case in which a judge ruled that cremation was not illegal, the first three cremations were held at Woking in 1885. In the following year there were 10.

Slowly, at first, the idea gained acceptance. More crematoria were built, in London and big provincial cities. By 1914 the annual number of cremations had risen to over 1,000. But there were still many churchgoers who opposed the practice. Shortly after the First World War, however, two Anglican bishops were cremated, which did much to change the attitude of many churchmen. By 1947 only just over 10 per cent of all the people who died were cremated. Since then there has been an enormous increase, so that now this method is used in almost half the total number of deaths. The practice was approved by the Pope in 1963.

One of the main claims made by its supporters is that it saves greatly-needed land. The cemeteries in Britain occupy about 25,000 acres and if no one were cremated they say that this area would need to be enlarged by about 500 acres every year. Up to December, 1964, there had been over 3 million cremations in Britain which, at an estimated 1,000 graves to an acre, has meant a saving in land of over 3,000 acres—a site big enough for 36,000 houses.

One of the greatest benefits produced by Western civilisation has been the improvement in personal and public health. Better sanitation, purer water and advances in medicine and surgery have given people the chance of living more healthy lives for a much longer period of time. Modern drugs and medical treatment have taken the pain and danger out of many, formerly often fatal, illnesses. Surgery and medicine now with their experimental transplants of various organs—kidneys, lungs, livers, hearts—are possibly on the verge of an equally significant breakthrough which could again revolutionise the lives of ordinary people. At the same time, the greater provision of social security in times of illness and of unemployment has removed much of the material anxieties from these periods of misfortune.

A General View

> The history of human society, when viewed in detail, is far more often darkened with tragedy, than it is lightened with hope. . . . Life for the nameless millions of mankind who have already lived and died has been wretched, short, hungry and brutal.—J. H. Plumb.

In the introduction to C. R. Boxer, *The Dutch Seaborne Empire, 1600–1800*, Hutchinson, 1965.

This book has tried to provide a survey of some of the most significant activities in the lives of ordinary people during the last 200 years or so. It has not attempted to look back upon their lives from a modern viewpoint but to visualise life as it must have appeared to them. The countless millions who lived and died in conditions of material wretchedness could do very little to change the conditions that society seemed to have imposed upon them. It was only in the most desperate circumstances that they rebelled or rioted, but these protests were mostly short-lived and usually unsuccessful. Much of this agitation, too, was not of their own making but conducted for the submerged poor by the compassionate middle class or by their more favoured peers who were blessed with more intelligence, determination and good fortune than they were themselves and had been able to rise above the class into which they had been born. Even the later developments of trade unions and socialist parties—whose activities did so much to alleviate the sufferings of the working class—were primarily controlled, initially at least, by the middle class, the more favoured artisans, and the more intelligent members of the mass of the working class itself.

For the majority of people the response to their problems was more often personal than social or political: the oblivion of drink, which until comparatively recent times was the major social problem; migration to one of the new industrial towns; voluntary emigration to the New World, so bright with hopes; or, for some minor offence, involuntary transportation to Australia, where, on release, many of the transported 'convicts' built a new and prosperous life in this land of undeveloped opportunities.

Although it is possible to describe the conditions of their lives, it is far more difficult to estimate what they thought and felt about them. For most of the period, there is no record of their feelings; many were illiterate and it was only the exceptional who could state what they felt. It is, however, probably true to say that they may have found their lives somewhat less depressing than we might do looking back on them. Lacking much perspective of freedom or of opportunity, they had to accept life as it was and to make the best of it. Their horizons were far more bounded than are ours. There were too many events, both personal and national, which were outside their control, or indeed, until quite recently, the control of anyone: many of their children died young, and nothing could be done to stop it; the weather was bad, so grain was short and prices high. They had less freedom and less sense of opportunity than we have, and therefore probably possessed a quiet and generally undisturbed acceptance of their fate which it is a little difficult for us to appreciate. The conditions under which they lived were too hard, their hours of work were too long, and the quality of the food they ate was too poor for them to feel much more than a dull care—relieved by rarer moments of celebration and happiness.

But the picture would be falsified if it were forgotten that these were all human beings with the same emotions, desires and needs as we have ourselves. It was simply that the opportunities for enjoyment and development then were much less than they are now; but they were no less eagerly sought and appreciated. Some of this feeling may be found in Somerville's description of his first visit to a fair, or in Mason's oblique references to the gossiping, tea-drinking dames.

In the eighteenth century and the early nineteenth century, the country with its closer-knit community and its natural course of changing seasons may have been in some ways a more pleasant and rewarding place to live in than the early industrial towns. It was only from about the 1880s that general conditions started to improve, gradually at first and then at an increasingly rapid pace. These improvements were not brought about by the activities of nineteenth century political and social reformers alone, but perhaps even more by the greater national wealth produced by the industrial revolution. There were reformers at work in all periods: no age has had a monopoly of compassion. There were many individuals in the eighteenth century who wanted to improve social conditions and did as much as they could towards it, and even governments were very much concerned about social conditions and would, for example, have solved the problem of abandoned and unwanted children if they had known how. But there was a general lack of knowledge and of opportunity; throughout history plain ignorance has been just as great, if not more, a cause of suffering as simple cruelty.

What permitted a general betterment of conditions were the improvements in technical, scientific and managerial techniques that we are accustomed to designate as the industrial revolution. Before that, there was simply not enough wealth to go round. The increased products of the factories permitted a population vastly increased in size to live at a higher standard. Although wealth is still unequally distributed in modern times, the actual proportion received by what used to be the working class has increased enormously (at the same time that received by the middle class has probably been somewhat reduced).

All change creates new problems and the modern age of industrial affluence is no exception. To mention only one example: the basic division of labour in factories has split up the whole work process into a series of repetitive routines. But when one looks back to life as it once was, it is apparent that modern problems are quite different in kind from those which once afflicted the vast mass of mankind. The restrictive poverty of the past, which affected the majority of the population, has now been narrowed down until it affects only a relatively small segment. And the concern and the ability to solve problems are now much more widespread than they ever were before. The most significant and the most encouraging feature of the history of the last 200 years is that, as Plumb so rightly says, the handful of favoured men who escaped the general misery and wretchedness of life is now at last becoming 'a significant proportion'.

BIBLIOGRAPHY

Books for Further Reading

J. J. and A. J. Bagley, *The English Poor Law*, Macmillan, 1966

Charles Booth, *Life and Labour of the People in London*, 1904

Asa Briggs, *Victorian Cities*, Penguin, 1968

Elizabeth Burton, *The Georgians at Home*, Longmans, 1967

G. Kitson Clark, *The Making of Victorian England*, Methuen, 1962

Courtney Dainton, *The Story of England's Hospitals*, Museum Press, 1961

Sir Jack Drummond and Anne Wilbraham, *The Englishman's Food*, Cape, 1957

Dorothy George, *England in Transition*, Penguin, 1953

L. G. Housden, *The Prevention of Cruelty to Children*, Cape, 1955

R. Huggett, *Shops*, Batsford, 1969

Henry Mayhew, *Mayhew's Characters*, edited by Peter Quennell, Spring Books, n.d.

B. R. Mitchell, *Abstract of British Historical Statistics*, Cambridge University Press, 1962

J. A. R. Pimlott, *The Englishman's Holiday*, Faber, 1947

J. H. Plumb, *England in the Eighteenth Century*, Penguin, 1955

W. J. Reader, *Life in Victorian England*, Batsford, 1964

Jack Simmons, *Transport*, Vista Books, 1962

Joseph Strutt, *The Sports and Pastimes of the People of England*, new edition enlarged by J. Charles Cox, Methuen, 1903

A. J. P. Taylor, *English History, 1914–1945*, Oxford, 1965

David Thomson, *England in the Nineteenth Century*, Penguin, 1963

David Thomson, *England in the Twentieth Century*, Penguin, 1966

Other Books Consulted

1. BIRTH AND EDUCATION

P. M. Braidwood, *The Domestic Management of Children*, 1874

John Brown, *A Memoir of Robert Blincoe*, 1832

John Brownlow, *The History and Design of the Foundling Hospital*, London, 1858

W. Cadogan, *An Essay upon Nursing and the Management of Children*, 1748

City of Bradford, *School Health Service Jubilee, 1908–1958*, n.d.

Henry Clark, *Sunday Schools and the Pew System*, Cheltenham, 1866

Harvey Graham, M.D., *Eternal Eve*, Hutchinson, 1960

Jonas Hanway, *A Candid Historical Account of the Hospital for the reception of Exposed and Deserted Young Children*, London, 1754

N. W. Hutchins, *4,000 Years of Infant Feeding*, The Chemist and Druggist, 1958

M. G. Jones, *The Charity School Movement*, Frank Cass, 1964

S. R. Townshend Mayer, *Who was the Founder of Sunday Schools?* London, 1880

S. R. Townshend Mayer, *The Origin and Growth of Sunday Schools in England*, London, 1878

Ministry of Education, *Report for the Year 1950*, HMSO, 1951

Ministry of Education, *Report for the Year 1947*, HMSO, 1948

C. Northcote, *Talks with Mothers*, London, 1894

Roger S. Peacock, *Pioneer of Boyhood*, Glasgow, 1954

George Reynolds, *The Madras School Grammar*, London, 1813

Alexander Sommerville, *The Autobiography of a Working Man*, London, 1848, also edited by John Carswell, Turnstile Press, 1951

Mrs. Furley Smith, *Child Life under Queen Victoria*, 1897

2. LOVE AND MARRIAGE

All About Etiquette, Ward Lock, 1875

Rev. J. O. Bevan, *Wooing and Wedding*, London, 1910

Commission on Divorce, 1850

Daniel Defoe, *Moll Flanders*, 1722

Robert Elliott, *The Gretna Green Memoirs*, 1842, with an introduction by the Rev. Caleb Brown

Nina Epton, *Love and the English*, Cassell, 1960

Rev. A. Keith, *Observations on the Act for Preventing Clandestine Marriages*, London, 1753

O. R. McGregor, *Divorce in England*, Heinemann, 1957

R. A. Melsom, *Courtship and Marriages Customs*, 1885

Registrar-General, *First Annual Report*, Parly. Papers, Vol. XVI, 1839

Registrar-General, *Statistical Review* for 1931, 1961 and 1962, HMSO

Samuel Richardson, *Letters written to and for Particular Friends on the most important occasions*, 3rd edition, London, 1746

Rev. R. Wilberforce Starr, *The Wedding Ring*, 1898

3. WORK AND LEISURE

A brief inquiry into Dwellings for the Industrial Class, London, 1851

A Statistical Account of the Township of Leeds, reprinted from the *Journal of the Statistical Society*, London, 1840

All About Etiquette, Ward Lock, 1875

An Enquiry into the State of the Manufacturing Population, London, 1831

William Belsham, *Remarks on the Bill for Better Support and Maintenance of the Poor*, London, 1797

Mary Carpenter, *Juvenile Delinquents*, London, 1853

George Crabbe, *Poetical Works*, Paris, 1829

Arthur C. David, *The Good Fight*, Baptist Union of Great Britain, n.d.

David Davies, *The Case of Labourers in Husbandry*, London, 1795

Enquire Within upon Everything, 1899

Dr. Tasker Evans, *Temperance in its Social Aspects*, 1877

P. Gaskell, *Artisans and Machinery*, 1836

P. Gaskell, *The Manufacturing Population of England*, 1833

Maurice Gorham, *Broadcasting and Television since 1900*, Andrew Dakers, 1952

A. H. Hill, *Vagrancy*, 1881

Octavia Hill, *Homes of the London Poor*, Macmillan, 1883

Hugh MacCallum, *The Distribution of the Poor in London*, 1883

W. Macqueen-Pope, *The Melodies Linger On*, W. H. Allen, n.d.

Simon Mason, *The Good and Bad Effects of Tea consider'd*, London, 1745

Ministry of Health, *Garden Cities and Satellite Towns*, Report of Departmental Committee, 1935

Ministry of Health, *Management of Municipal Housing Estates*, 1938

W. C. Preston, *Light and Shade*, 1885

W. C. Preston, *The Bitter Cry of Outcast London*, 1883

Robert Redmayne, editor, *Ideals in Industry*, 1951

William Rivington, *Past and Present State of St. Pancras*, London, 1845

R. H. Sherard, *The White Slaves of England*, 1897

The Economy of Cottage Life, London, 1847

The Gin Shop, Cheap Repository for Moral Tracts, n.d.

The Jubilee of George the Third, London, 1887

The World Film Encyclopaedia, Amalgamated Press, 1933

4. CRIME AND WARS

A Soldier's Journal, 1770

A Treatise on the Police and Crimes of the Metropolis, London, 1829

John Ashton, *The Fleet*, 1888

Essays on Duty and Discipline, Cassell, 1910

Sir Lionel Wray Fox, *The English Prison*, 1952

John Howard, *The State of Prisons in England and Wales*, 3rd edition, 1784

—, *The Soldier in Peace and War*, 1855

Prisons and Borstals, HMSO, 1950

Reports of the Governor, Chaplain and Surgeon of the Leeds Borough Gaol, Leeds, 1855

Gordon Rose, *The Struggle for Penal Reform*, Stevens and Sons, 1961

The Probation Service, HMSO, 1952

Warwick Wroth, *The London Pleasure Gardens*, Macmillan, 1896

5. SICKNESS AND MOURNING

Sir Edwin Chadwick, *Report for Poor Law Commissioners on an inquiry into Sanitary State of the Labouring Population of Great Britain*, 1842

Sir Edwin Chadwick, *The Practice of Interment in Towns*, 1843

Daniel Hack Tuke, *Chapters in the History of the Insane*, 1882

HAPPENINGS

1. BIRTH AND EDUCATION

The Georgian Age

1741 Foundling Hospital opened

1749 British Lying-in Hospital opened

1752 General Lying-in Hospital opened

1780 Robert Raikes and the Rev. Thomas Stock start Sunday school in Gloucester.

The Years of Growth

1802 First Factory Act

1810 Madras, or monitorial, system of education starts to expand

1811 Church of England National Society for education founded

1833 Factory inspectors appointed

1842 Women and young children banned from working underground in coal mines

1867 Children under eight banned from working in agricultural gangs

1870 Education Act

Modern Times

1883 Boys' Brigade started

1888 National Society for Prevention of Cruelty to Children founded

1890 First school medical officer

1893 School leaving age raised from 10 to 11

1899 School leaving age raised to 12

1906 'Official' school dinner service started

1907 First infant welfare centre

1907 'Free' places provided at grammar schools

1908 Boy Scouts movement founded

1918 School leaving age raised to 14

1947 School leaving age raised to 15

2. LOVE AND MARRIAGE

The Georgian Age

1753 Lord Hardwicke's Marriage Act

The Years of Growth

1836 Catholics and Dissenters allowed to be married in own place of worship Register office marriages legalised

1857 Divorce courts set up

1878 Separation orders for wives

Modern Times

1886 Permitted hours for church weddings extended to 3 p.m.

1923 Change in divorce law in women's favour

1929 Minimum age for marriage raised to 16

1937 Sir Alan Herbert's divorce law

3. WORK AND LEISURE

The Georgian Age

1751 Gin duty increased

1787 MCC formed

1795 Bill to secure minimum wage defeated

1795 Speenhamland system of poor relief starts

1805 Primitive Methodist Church founded

The Years of Growth

1818 Government grant for building churches in towns

1824 Combination Acts repealed

1830 Unlicensed beer houses permitted

1831 Lord's Day Observance Society started

1832 Preston Temperance League formed

1833 Grand National Consolidated Trades Union

1834 Poor Law Amendment Act

1835 Bull-baiting made illegal

1847 Ten-hour act

1847 Band of Hope formed

1850 First practical sewing machine

1861 Post Office Savings Bank

1863 Football Association formed

1868 Trades Union Congress met

1869 Beer houses had to be licensed again

1871 Bank Holiday Act

1878 Consolidating Factory Act

1878 Salvation Army formed

1881 First issue of *Titbits*

Modern Times

1885 Report of Royal Commission on housing

1886 Bill to enfranchise women defeated

1894 First Lyons' teashop

1896 First issue of *Daily Mail*

1896 First British car; speed limit raised from 4 m.p.h.

1903 First garden city Workers' Educational Association formed First issue of *Daily Mirror*

1906 Permanent waving of hair started

1908 Old age pensions started

1909 Labour exchanges set up

1911 National Insurance Act

1918 Women over 30 given vote

1919 Government gives councils subsidies to build council houses

1922 First BBC broadcast

1924 Housing Act

1929 Youth Hostels Association founded

1936 TV starts

1937 Butlin's holiday camp opened

4. CRIME AND WARS

The Georgian Age

1790 John Howard dies

1805 London horse patrol starts

1813 Elizabeth Fry starts work at Newgate Prison

The Years of Growth

1829 Metropolitan Police formed

1842 Pentonville Prison opened

1856 Police Act

1868–74 Army reforms

1877 Board of Prison Commissioners take over country gaols

Modern Times

1887 Probation for first offenders instituted

1895 Inquiry into prison conditions

1907 Official probation service starts

1908 Borstal system instituted

1908 Juvenile courts started

1925 Probation officers made compulsory

1948 Criminal Justice Act

1848 Public Health Act

1859 Metropolitan Free Drinking Fountain Association founded

1860 Florence Nightingale Training School opens

1865 Main London sewers completed

Modern Times

1885 First cremations at Woking

1895 X-rays discovered

1942 Beveridge Report

1948 National Health Service starts

5. SICKNESS AND MOURNING

The Georgian Age

1802 London Fever Hospital opened

1815 Inquiry into conditions at 'Bedlam'

The Years of Growth

1832 Private cemetery opens at Kensal Green

1834 Ancient Order of Foresters started

1842 Chadwick's report on sanitation

1843 Chadwick's report on burials

1846 First operation in Britain using anaesthetics

INDEX